The Diary of Civil War

Private Richard Dodge

15th Regiment
New Hampshire Volunteers

Compiled, Edited and Annotated

by

Dr. Leonard J. Nyberg, Jr., SUVCW
Camp Five – New Hampshire
Camp Seven – Rhode Island

Railroad Street Press
394 Railroad Street, Suite 2
St. Johnsbury, VT 05819

The Diary of Civil War Private Richard Dodge

15th Regiment
New Hampshire Volunteers

Printed in the United States of America

Cover Design by Michelle Linell
www.eyedesignsgraphics.com

ISBN 9781936711055

Additional copies of this book may be obtained through your local bookstore, on-line, or directly from the author:

Dr. Leonard J. Nyberg, Jr.
www.w1ljn.com
125 Savageville Road
Lisbon, New Hampshire 03585

Or by email at: nyberg1@roadrunner.com

Railroad Street Press
394 Railroad Street, Suite 2
St. Johnsbury, VT 05819
(802) 748-3551
www.railroadstreetpress.com

Dedication

This book has been compiled in grateful recognition of the valiant and self-sacrificing service to their country of those brave men who went from the small towns and villages of New Hampshire, to join the forces of the Union during the Civil War. Some returned, some did not. However, all who returned bore the physical and mental scars of the horror of war for many years thereafter. May none ever be forgotten: ***"Requiem aeternam donna eis, Domine, et lux perpetua luceat eis."***

I would like to thank all those who assisted me in preparing this work, Doreen Kaspszak for sharing her great-grandfather's diary with me. Andrea Fitzgerald, who spent countless hours reading and editing the manuscript; her suggestions and guidance were invaluable. To my wife Dawn, who helped me greatly with her computer expertise and loving support.

To Michelle Linell, whose talent and artistic skills in the graphic arts made the cover design of this book a reality.

Foreword

The Civil War began in 1861 and continued until the surrender of the Confederate Army in 1865. During that period thousands of men from both sides fought and died. The towns of Lisbon, Lyman, and Landaff, New Hampshire, sent over 188 young men into service, and forty (21%) died, 43 (22%) were disabled and about 26 were reported as deserters. The remainder were either discharged or mustered out without physical injury. Essentially, over forty percent of those sent were either killed, died from disease, or disabled.

Richard Dodge was from Lyman, New Hampshire and wrote his diary during the period from January, 1863 through July, 1863. His enlistment began in Concord, New Hampshire and from there the regiment traveled by train to Connecticut where they boarded a steamer to New York. On December 11, 1862, Richard's Company "C" boarded the steamship *Cambria* and proceeded along the east coast and then along the south coast of Florida before heading to Ship Island to take on coal. From there they headed for the Mississippi River and steamed up river to Carrollton, Louisiana where they disembarked at 3 p. m. on December 26, 1862. The entire voyage took fifteen days.

Company "C," among others in the regiment, made camp at Camp Mansfield in Carrollton before moving north to Camp Parapet. The first few months in camp were less than exciting, but that would soon change.

My wife and I have followed Richard and his comrades through their journeys from New Orleans, through Carrollton, Camp Parapet, Baton Rouge, Springfield Landing and Port Hudson. We have toured the Port Hudson battlefield three times. During our last visit, Marvin McGraw, a Civil War enthusiast and friend from Baton Rouge, gave us a personal guided tour of that portion of the battlefield outside the State Historic Site boundaries.

We have walked where Richard and his comrades have walked, and we attempted to imagine what they saw and experienced. We have visited the Port Hudson National Military Cemetery where Richard's tent-mate and friend Isaac Smith was buried in an unmarked grave along with others from their regiment and hundreds more from other regiments.

I am in sincere hopes that this book will become an historical reference for those who enjoy reading and studying about the day-to-day lives of typical Civil War soldiers and the joys, sorrows and hardships that they endured in their fight for their country and their beliefs.

Table of Contents

INTRODUCTION

PRIVATE RICHARD DODGE DIARY, ANNOTATED

Richard Dodge was from Lyman, New Hampshire and a member of the Fifteenth Regiment, New Hampshire Volunteers. The following passages from his diary focus on his activities and the activities of his comrades during their ninety day enlistment, during which they saw action in the Battle of Port Hudson, Louisiana. Where appropriate, I have compared or embellished Richard's comments with some of those in Charles McGregor's diary published in the *History of the Fifteenth Regiment N.H. Volunteers,* published by the Fifteenth Regiment Association, 1900.

Richard. Dodge of the
Town of Lyman State
of Newhampshire and
County of Grafton. now
A, member of the
Newhampshire Vollenteers
15th Regt Co. C. Drummer
Dated January the 1st 1863
Neworlens City
State of Louisinia

Richard Dodge

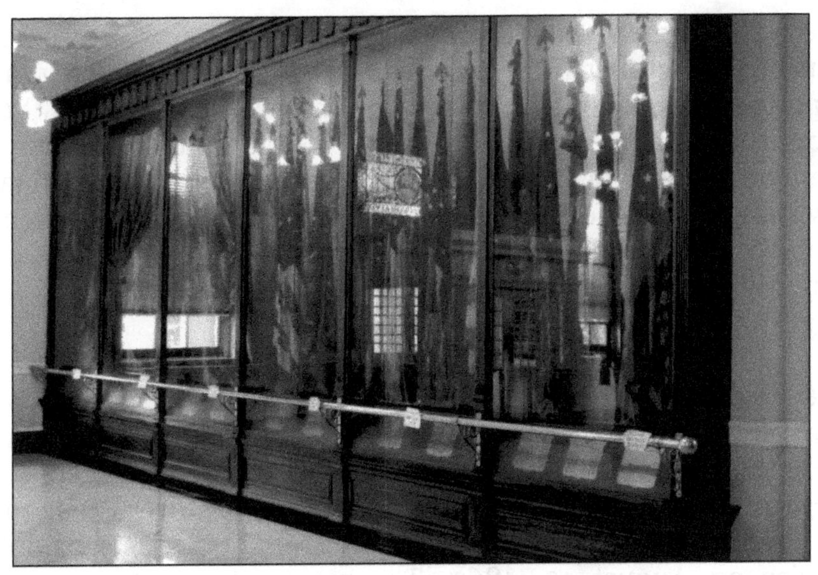

New Hampshire State Regimental Flag Display – State House, Concord, New Hampshire

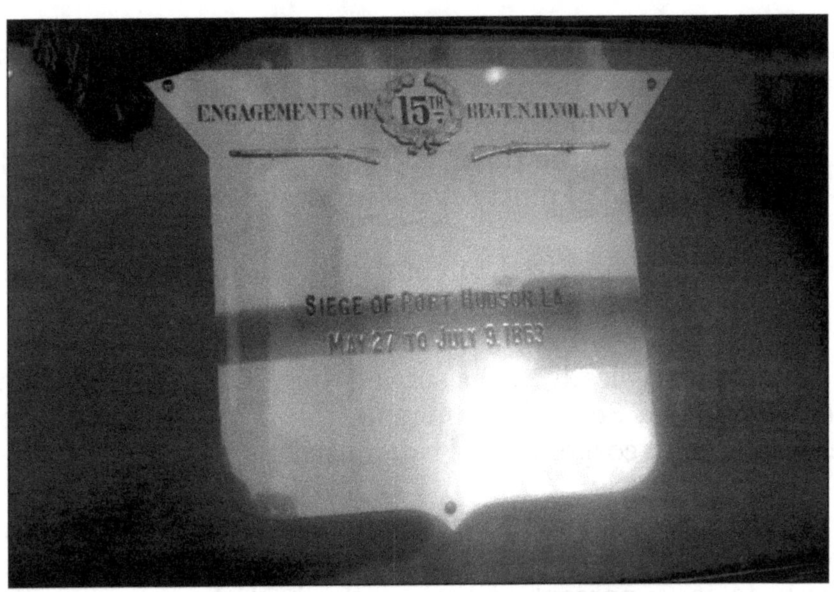

Plaque – 15th New Hampshire Volunteers – State House, Concord, New Hampshire
(Photos by the author)

The 15th Regiment New Hampshire Volunteers was organized at Concord in October 1862 for nine months' service. The regiment departed the state on November 13th and proceeded to New York. From there they proceeded to New Orleans, Louisiana, arriving there on the 26th of December. They were attached to Sherman's Division, Department of the Gulf, until January, 1863; then 1st Brigade, 2nd Division, 19th Army Corps, Army of the Gulf until July, 1863; then 2nd Brigade, 3rd Division, 19th Army Corps, until August, 1863.

The regiment moved from Carrollton, Louisiana to Camp Parapet on January 28th and were on duty there until May. From there they moved to Springfield Landing and then engaged in the Siege of Port Hudson until the surrender in July. From there they returned to Concord, New Hampshire and mustered out of service on August 13, 1863. The regiment lost twenty-seven Enlisted men killed and mortally wounded, and 134 Enlisted men by disease. Total – 161.

Richard Dodge enlisted on October 10, 1862 as a musician and was mustered into Company "C," 15th Regiment, New Hampshire Volunteers, on October 18, 1863. He was the company drummer and 28 years old at the time. At the time of his enlistment, his company consisted of ninety-five officers and men.

A Company is authorized to consist of the following numbers:
100 men = two platoons = four sections = eight squads

A company typically consists of one Captain, one First Lieutenant, one Second Lieutenant, one First Sergeant, four Sergeants, eight corporals and two musicians.

Note that these are authorized numbers and many Civil War units, when in the field, frequently operated at anywhere from twenty to forty percent of their authorized strength. Further, because of casualties these units many times were commanded by officers one or two grades below that authorized. It was not uncommon, particularly in remote areas, that these numbers frequently demonstrated considerable variation.

Local men in Richard's Company "C" included the following:

From Lyman:

George W. Bailey, age 27
Charles Cram, age 29
James H. Garland, age 39
John W. Millen, age 22
Amos V. Parker, first corporal, age 37
Benjamin Bailey, second corporal, age 40; severely wounded on May 27, 1863.
Richard Dodge, musician, age 28
John A. Powers, age 27
Isaac Smith, age 29.

From Landaff:

John Bishop, third sergeant, age 44
Harrison C. Howland, appointed wagoner, age 22; wounded May 27, 1863
Calvin J. Carpenter, age 20
Henry W. Howland, third corporal, age 20
Alson S. Little, age 18
Daniel Spooner, age 23
William H. Young, age 19
Francis A. Oaks, age 22
John Stuart, age 44.

The ages of men in Richard's Company range from nineteen to forty-four with an average age of twenty-nine; ages of Civil War soldiers varied widely, young boys of twelve through seventeen were common and men in their sixties were not unheard of; there is a report of a man eighty years, however, he was not assigned to combat duty.

On December 11, 1862, the company boarded the steamship "Cambria" and cruised south with stops at Fortress Monroe, Virginia, Ship Island, Mississippi, and New Orleans, Louisiana.

On December 26 Richard and his comrades arrived at Carrollton, Louisiana on the "Cambria," at which point they joined the regiment and camped at Camp Mansfield in Carrollton, the camp was formerly Camp Williams but the name was changed to Camp Mansfield by general orders, December 27, 1862.

The camp is described by Charles McGregor as follows: "Our camp at Carrollton – 'Mansfield' – is a little white city on a broad, level green, fronting on the celebrated shell road or Carrollton avenue. It is a hive of industry, where universal order reigns and discipline, as with the proverbial bee. It is very beautiful by day and especially charming by night, when all its lights are trimmed and burning. Its aspect is one of peace, and the land and climate semi-tropical and delightful. Our camp is only one of many in the vicinity of New Orleans; it is just on the margin of Carrollton. The principal street of Carrollton is Levee street. The river front is a busy scene; mighty fleets are there passing to and fro, lying quietly at anchor in the stream or moored to the shore, and discharging troops, freights and munitions of war in prodigious quantities. The river when full rises to the very top of the levee, which here is an immense and continuous bank of earth some twelve or fifteen feet above the land. It is a much frequented promenade on its broad top, and at its foot a small stream of leach water runs in a ditch."

The following order of calls and sanitary orders in relation to cleanliness was soon promulgated:

Drummers' call at daybreak
Reveille, 15 minutes later
Police call immediately after reveille
Surgeon's call, 7:30 A.M.
Breakfast, 8:00 A.M.
First call for parade and company inspection, 9:15 A.M.
Regimental Parade, 9:30 A.M.
Drill call, 10:00 A.M.
Recall from drill, 12 Noon
Dinner call, 12:30 P.M.
Fatigue call, 1:00 P.M.
First call for guard mount, 3:00 P.M.
Second call for guard mount, 3:15 P.M.
Recall from fatigue one half hour before retreat
Drummers' call, 15 minutes before retreat
Retreat parade, sundown.
Drummers' call, 8:15 P.M.

Tattoo, 8:30 P.M.
Taps, 15 minutes after tattoo.
Sunday inspection, first call 9 A. M.
Sunday inspection, second call, 9.15 A. M.
Sunday church call, 11 A. M.

All other necessary calls will be sounded under brigade or regimental commanders.

This order was issued by Brigadier General T. W. Sherman, Wickham Hoffman, A.A.G. It illustrates what the general routine of duty was during the month. It does not show, however, the menial drudgery of camp life – the cooking, the hewing of wood and drawing of water, the endless scouring of guns and buttons and brasses with emery paper and other polishes, and the blacking of boots, etc., which occupied nearly every spare moment of time.

EXTRACT FROM SANITARY ORDER

"Officers are directed to see (1st) that soldiers wash the whole person at least once a week; (2d) keep their clothes as clean as possible, and air their blankets every day in fair weather; (3d) that the grounds about the tents are not broken, and company streets and grounds are kept scrupulously clean and neat. (4th) Officers are forbidden to drink any but cistern or river water, and are advised to drink as little as they can do with. (5th) All are advised to eat but one orange daily and at most not over two. (6th) All night air is to be avoided as much as possible. (7th) Abstain from eating except at meals. (8th) None will be allowed to wear his hair or beard long, and must wash the head thoroughly every day. (9th) Abstain from cider and whiskey, especially the latter. (10th) Not to be out of the tent after nightfall without the overcoat on."

SANITARY INSPECTOR'S REPORT.

15th Reg. N. H. Vols., ... 186 .

Companies.	Officers' tents.	Grounds.	Soldiers' tents.	Grounds.	Personal cleanliness.
A					
B					
C					
D					
E					
F					
G					
H					
I					
K					

Remarks.

Perfect cleanliness and neatness will be marked 1
A slight defect in any respect will be marked 1½
And so on up to 5, which will call for a public reprimand and punishment.

By command of
COL. JOHN W. KINGMAN.

EDWARD E. PINKHAM,
Adjutant.

Sanitary Inspector's Report

The order of calls and sanitary order on the previous page describes the day-to-day activities of Richard and his companions while in the New Orleans area and his diary describes events that took place during his service in Louisiana. The diary begins on January 1, 1863 and continues through Friday July 31, 1863. Although some of the entries express daily routine and, in his words, little of interest to report, I have included each page in its' entirety.

I have made every effort to ensure the accuracy of my notations, however, some errors or omissions may unavoidably occur.

THE DIARY

Chapter One
January, 1863

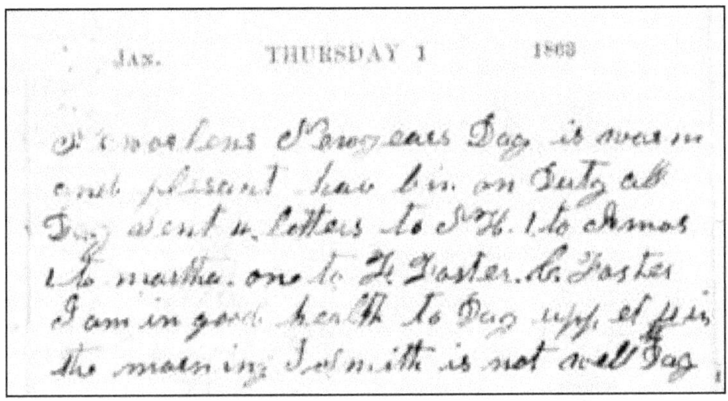

JAN. THURSDAY 1 1863

January 1, 1863 – New Orleans New years Day is warm and plesant have been on Duty all Day Sent 4 letters to NH. 1 to Amos 1 to Martha one to F. Foster. C. Foster. I am in good health today up at 4 in the morning. I Smith is not well today.

Isaac Smith is referenced many times in the diary; Isaac was from Lyman and a member of Company "C," New Hampshire 15th Infantry; more about him later.

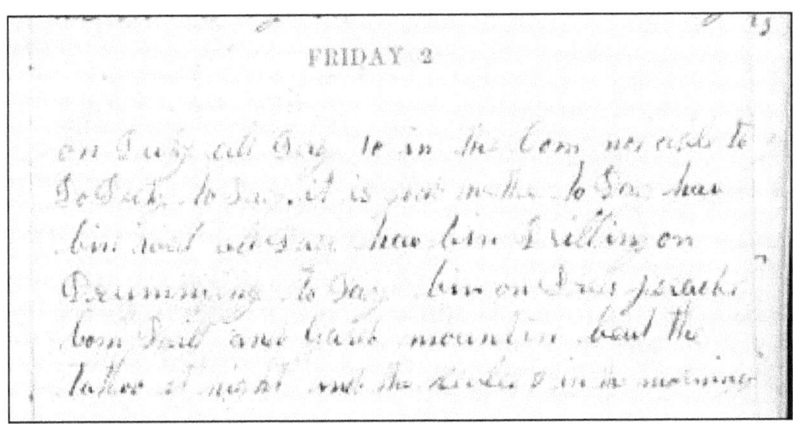

FRIDAY 2

January 2, 1863 – on Duty all Day 10 in the Com not able to Do Duty to Day it is good wether to Day have bin well all Day have bin Drilling on Drumming to Day bin on Dress parade Com[pany] Drill and Gard mountin beat the tattoo at night and the revele in the morning

SATURDAY 3

January 3, 1863 – on Duty all Day to Day it has rained to Day a little have bin well all Day but not able to Do Duty to Day all well in our Camp to Day 1 yest 1 to Day no letters for me to Day but a lot for Co C Some 4 or 5 a peace

JAN. SUNDAY 4 1863

January 4, 1863 – well to Day attended to the Devine services in the forenoon went upp to Camp parapet in the afternoon to find Unekle Josephs Grave Returned et 5 o clock we had a very heavey thunder shower last night and it rained very hard.

Camp Parapet was located north of Richard's camp at Carrollton – Uncle Joseph was Private Joseph Foster, more on him later.

McGregor recalls: "Sunday services; text, Matt. 7:29 – 'He taught them as one having authority, and not as the Scribes.'"

MONDAY 5

January 5, 1863 – to Day is very pleasant and warm hav bin on Duty all Day 2 excused from Duty to Day all is well in our tent but C. B. Ella Dress parade and Battalion Drill Gard mountain Drill Co Drill all to Day

TUESDAY 6

January 6, 1863 – to Day is plesant hav bin on Duty all Day received new guns for the Co. I Received one par of pants one……….

McGregor writes: "The Belgian muskets, which we brought from Concord, are exchanged for Enfield rifles... The 'Belgians' were old, and converted from flintlocks; the Enfields were second hand, but good."

American manufacturers of firearms were not able to meet the demand for weapons during the first part of the Civil war; accordingly, it was necessary to look to the European market for firearms. The Belgian musket varied so widely in caliber and in quality that the typical Civil War soldier replaced them as expeditiously as possible when the opportunity arose.

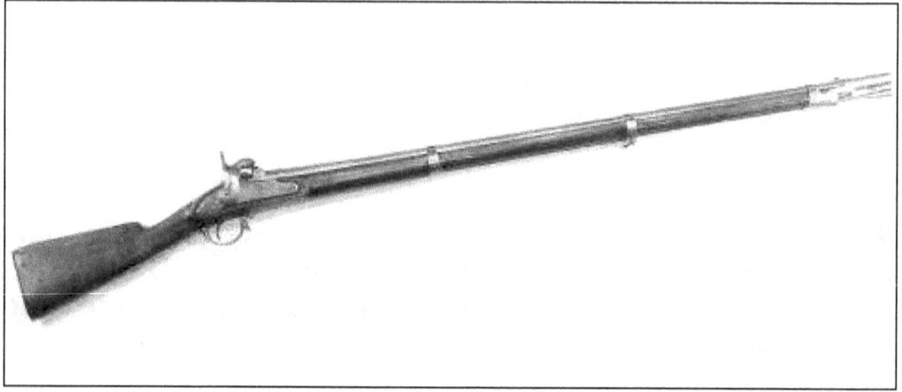

Typical Belgian Musket

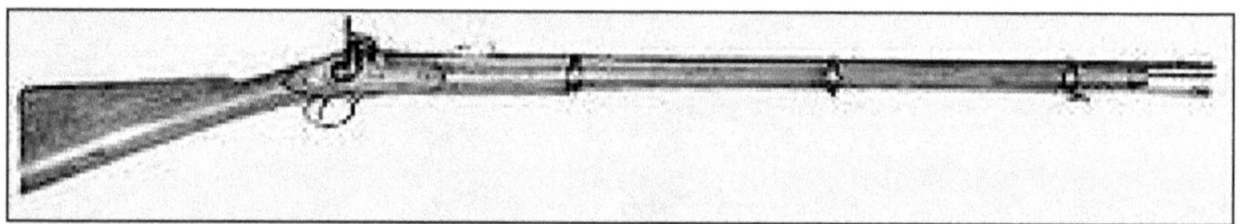

Typical Enfield Musket

The Enfield 1853 Rifle-Musket was also used by both the North and the South in the Civil War and was the second most widely used infantry weapon in that war. It was surpassed only by the 1861 Springfield Rifled Musket. The Confederates imported more Enfields during the course of the war than any other small arm, purchasing them primarily from private contractors and gun runners when the British government refused to sell them arms after it became obvious that the Confederacy could not win the war. It has been estimated that over 900,000 Enfield rifles were imported to America.

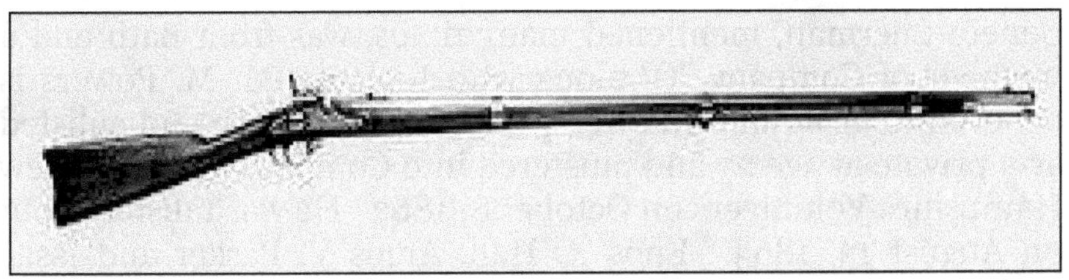

Typical Springfield Musket

Almost one million .58 caliber Springfield muskets were manufactured by the Springfield Armory including those built by twenty licensed contractors. This musket had a maximum range of 1,000 yards and an experienced soldier could fire this weapon at a rate of two to three rounds per minute.

JAN. WEDNESDAY 7 1863

THURSDAY 8

January 7, 1863 – to Day is Cool but pleasant have Drummed all the Calls to Day to the guard house 3 of our Com gon to the horspittle all well in our tent. Benera Sherman, M. M. Powers, A. V. Parker, Isaac Smith, E. K. Hall and others all on guard to night for fear of Rebils.

Benera Sherman, mentioned many times, was from Bath and a member of Company "C" along with Richard; M. M. Powers is believed to be John M. Powers, who was from Bath and enlisted as a private at age 27 and mustered into Company "C," 15th New Hampshire Volunteers on October 8, 1862. He was mustered out on August 13, 1863. Enos K. Hall, Amos V. Parker and Issac Smith were from Lyman and also members of Company "C." More on them later.

A tent was made up of five men, their guns were stacked at the back and their belts, cartridge boxes and cap pouches were suspended from each bayonet, knapsacks were frequently used as pillows and, often, bayonets were stuck in the ground and used as candle holders.

McGregor recalls: "What is that lone drum beating so early? It is the drummer's call – the morn is up. In fifteen minutes more all the drummers – one from each company – meet near the colonel's quarters, and suddenly strike up a stirring and animated drumming that would alarm the sleeping world; it is the reveille."

(Recall that Richard Dodge was the drummer for Company "C")

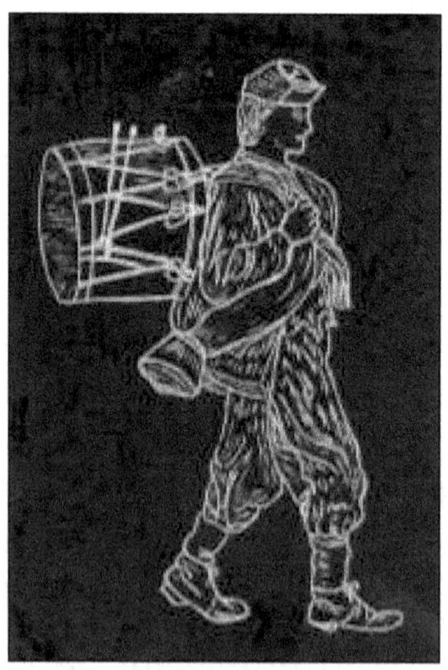

Company Drummer
(Author's collection)

Tent City
(Author's collection)

Rebils THURSDAY 8

to Day we mooved from Camp mansfie
Down to the vilage Com E and B are
on provose gard we hav taken in
5 Rebil prissners to Day all well
in our tent it is pleasant and warm
to Day hav bin on Duty all Day..

January 8, 1863 – to Day we mooved from Camp Mansfield Down to the vilage Com. E and B are on provose gard we hav taken in 5 Rebil prisseners to Day all well in our tent it is pleasant and warm to Day hav bin on Duty all Day...

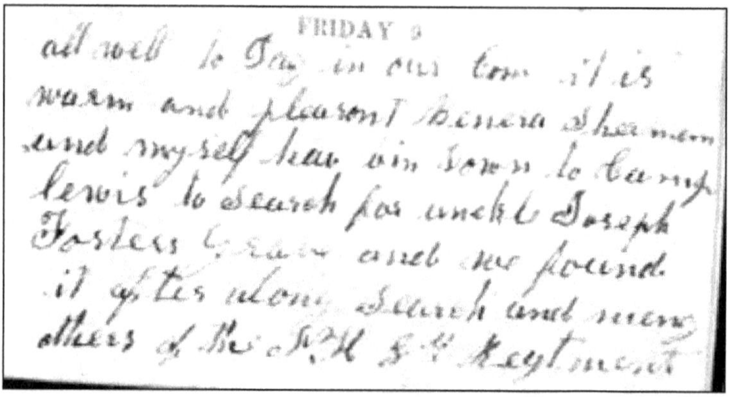

January 9, 1863 – all well to day in our Com[pany] it is warm and pleasant Benera Sherman and myself have been down to Camp Lewis to search for uncle Joseph Foster's grave and we found it after a long search and many others of the NH 8th Regtment.

Joseph Foster was from Lyman and enlisted as a private at the age of 33 and mustered into Company "H" on December 20, 1861. His records indicate that he died of disease on October 29, 1862 at Camp Kearney, Louisiana. Camp Lewis was located on the former Burthe and Foucher plantation and on the Carrollton and New Orleans Railway line adjacent to the settlement of Greenville and about one and one-half miles below Carrollton. The camp was named after Major General John L. Lewis, commanding general of the First Louisiana Militia. At one point the camp was also called Camp Kearney. At the present time the former camp is the Audubon Park (Arrow).

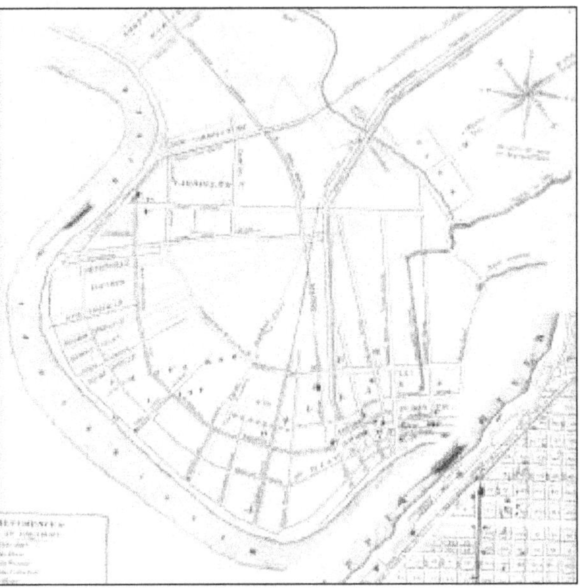

The area that is described as City Park was the Foucher Plantation, which was first acquired by Louis Foucher in 1793. He died in 1832. Shortly before the Civil War, the plantation was abandoned by his son. During the Civil War, both Confederate and Union units occupied the site, which the Confederates named Camp Lewis. After the fall of New Orleans in 1862 Union forces under the command of General Benjamin Butler moved in and built a temporary hospital called Camp Sedgwick.

Two newspaper articles published in the New Orleans Daily Crescent speak of the camp:

In the June 15, 1861 issue: "New Camp Ground – Generals Lewis and Forstall have selected ground for a camp for our Horse Brigade at Foucher's Plantation, on the Carrollton Railroad, in Jefferson Parish. The troops will be supplied with water by aqueduct from river."

In the June 24th issue: "Orleans Artillery Battalion........[A]fter the ceremony, the Artillerists took up their line of march for Camp Lewis......Yesterday the Artillerists were visited by great numbers of people. The camp is on a large open field in Rickerville, on the Carrollton Railroad, with rows of trees along the sides, affording a pleasant shade during the hot hours of the day."

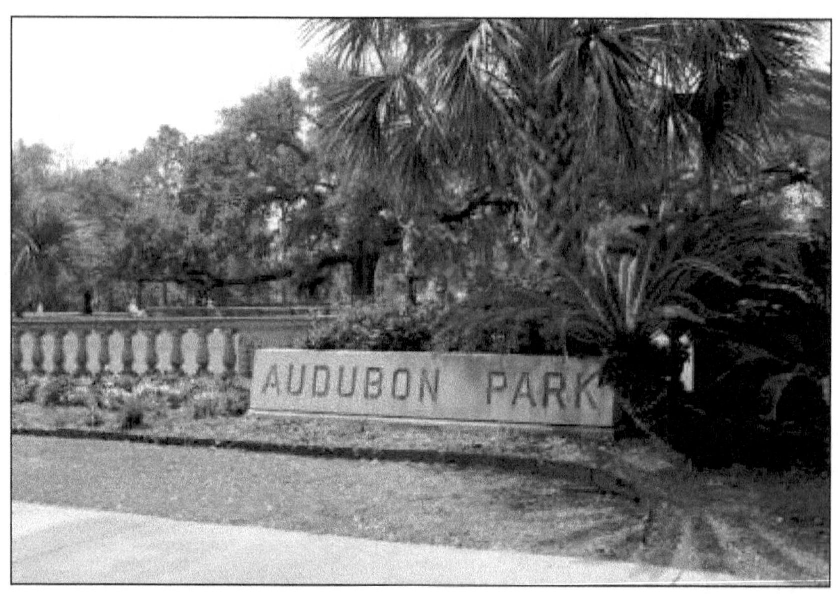

Park entrance as it appeared in 2009
(Photograph by the Author)

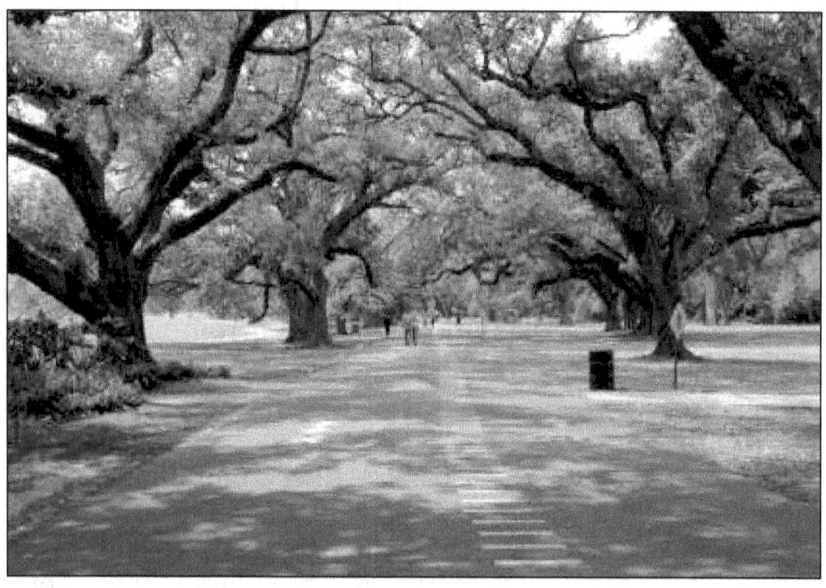

Park Trees
Many of these were probably there during the time of Camp Lewis
(Photograph by the Author)

JAN. SATURDAY 10 1863

is warm and pleasant hav bin on Duty all Day no news of any importence all is well in our tent To Day no news from home yet feel rather lonely about it kinder Down harted to Day

January 10, 1863 – is warm and pleasant hav bin on Duty all Day no news of any importence all is well in our tent to Day no news from home yet feel rather lonely about it kinder Down harted to Day

"No news from home......kinder Down harted..." This entry reflected the mood of many soldiers, particularly those that were away from home for the first time. Loneliness such as this was prevalent during the Civil War. Most soldiers had never been away from home before nor had many traveled very far from home before their enlistment. All of a sudden they found themselves far away from their friends, family and familiar surroundings, and this, along with poor food, unhealthy conditions, and fear of the unknown, led to boredom and homesickness.

Letters from home were the general cure for the "sickness" and many thousands of letters passed through the postal services of the times. Letters from home were essentially the only contact that soldiers had with their loved-ones, and when those letters did not arrive signs of homesickness were sure to follow. In extreme cases, homesickness sometimes led to desertion, particularly when bad news came from home.

Anyone who has been away from home for camp at an early age can easily relate to this malady.

Letters, and sometimes newspapers from home arrived by numerous methods, an Army Mail Wagon is pictured above. Regiments generally had mail clerks who had the responsibility to see that mail was received and distributed to the men, duties also included forwarding mail from the front to the folks at home.

SUNDAY 11

all is well hav bin in the tent
all Day nothing to Do to Day only
night and morning I had to beat
the Revelie and tattoo and taps
has bin very warm to Day one
Steemer from NY but no mail for
us bad luck to the Ship

January 11, 1863 – all is well hav bin in the tent all Day nothing to Do to Day only night and morning I had to beat the Revelie and tattoo and taps has bin very warm to Day one Steemer from NY but no mail for us bad luck

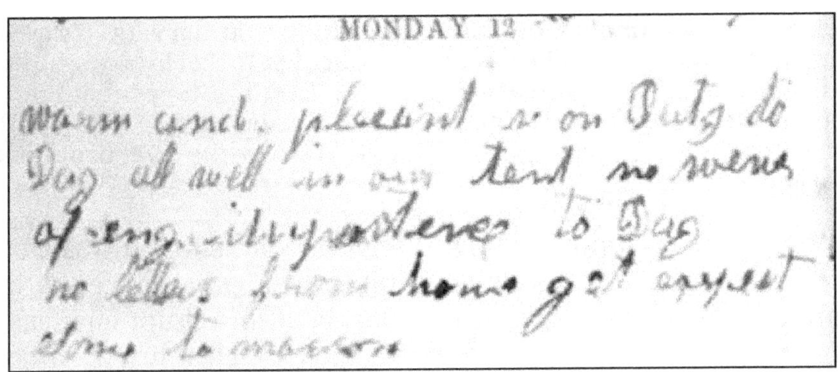
MONDAY 12

January 12, 1863 – warm and plesant on Duty to Day all well in our tent no news of any importence to Day no letters from home yet expect some to morrow.

JAN. TUESDAY 13 1863

January 13, 1863 – am not very well today but do my duty all day - one man of Company "B" by the name of Charles Perkins was buried to day the first man that has died in the Regt. Several others quite sick to day.

Charles G. Perkins was from Haverhill and enlisted as a Private at age 31 and mustered into Company "B," 15th New Hampshire Volunteers on October 8, 1862. His records indicate that he died of disease on January 12, 1863 at Carrollton, Louisiana.

McGregor's comments on the same day: "January 13, Tuesday. Warm and pleasant. The funeral of Charles G. Perkins took place to-day at 4 o'clock in the afternoon; the first military burial in the regiment. It cast a gloom over the whole camp. The entire regiment was formed with reversed arms while the procession passed."

Sickness was common among the Union soldiers and was called by several names including camp fever, swamp fever and climactic fever, essentially it was the result of abrupt changes in temperature, dampness and bugs, lack of cleanliness, among other things, indigenous to the area. A frequent symptom was diarrhea, and although many were successfully treated, in some cases the malady was fatal and in others a call for discharge was necessary due to disability.

Chronic diarrhea, typhoid fever and dysentery accounted for about one-half of the total deaths from disease during the Civil War. It is estimated that over six hundred thousand troops died during the war and of this total approximately two hundred thousand were the result of wounds received in battle and the remainder were the result of disease.

A typical Civil War Field Hospital – Baton Rouge, Louisiana (Author's collection)

McGregor describes conditions and a makeshift hospital in Carrollton:

> **"Very heavy rain and mud knee deep; wind blows at night. The sick in the hospital are, many of them, delirious; the disease is called camp fever, swamp fever, or climactic fever.... The hospital at Carrollton was a mansion house, which had been deserted by the Confederates; it contained six or eight large beds, with canopy tops and mosquito screens; beside these there were thirty or forty cots. There were screens on the windows, and everything was clean and white as snow. It was soon, however, found inadequate, and the overflow was, in some instances, very poorly quartered. A man would be stricken suddenly with these fevers, and in an half hour his eyes would turn yellow and vomiting spells would ensue; the skin would become so hot so as to burn the hand like a hot gun barrel. In one hour the temperature would increase to 108 degrees under the tongue, and soon the skin would also turn yellow, and in many incidences, unless relief was afforded, the victim would die within a day's time."**

Not all hospital facilities were as "sophisticated" as McGregor described, many times the "hospital facilities" were no more than tents, or, on the battlefield, simply dugouts in the sides of hills.

WEDNESDAY 14

January 14, 1863 – I am well to Day it has bin a rainey day all well in our tent no news of any importence have been on duty all Day it has been rather cool here to Day hav taken 3 prisoners to Day

THURSDAY 15

January 15, 1863 – am well hav bin on Duty all Day all well in our tent no letters yet no news of any importence

McGregor writes: "January 15, Thursday. Heavy rain and high wind; mercury at 72 degrees. Paid off to January 1 in bright, new greenbacks, worth about forty cents on the dollar, which would make a soldier's pay in good money about five dollars per month or sixty dollars per annum, with clothing and blankets deducted from that."

JAN. FRIDAY 16 1863

January 16, 1863 – all well with pleasent weather to Day no news to Day Com has Received some letters had not eny myself two men killed by a negro woman on the other side of the River.

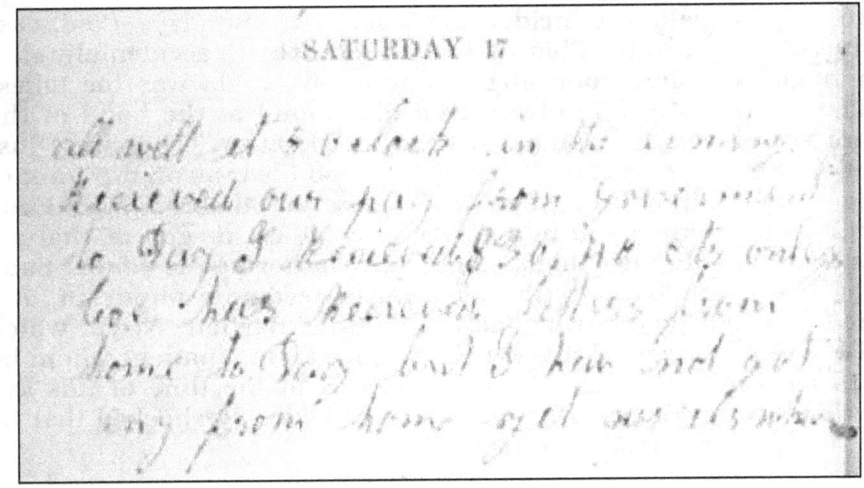

SATURDAY 17

January 17, 1863 – all well at 8 o clock in the evening Recieved our pay from Government to Day I recieved $30. 40 cts only Co e has Recieved letters from home to Day but I hav not yet any from home or elsewhere.

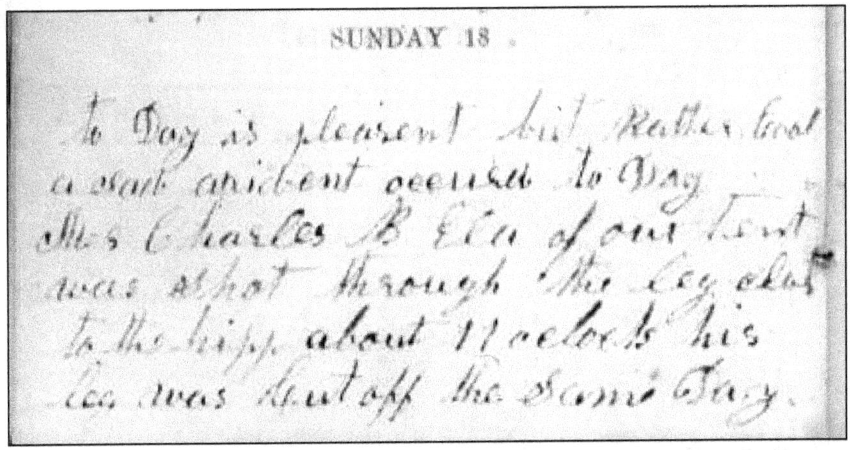

SUNDAY 18

January 18, 1863 – to Day is pleasant but Rather Cool a sad axident occurred to Day Charles B. Ela of our tent was shot through the leg close to the hip about 11 o'clock his leg was cut off the same day.

McGregor recalls the incident: "January 18, Sunday. Cold, east wind blowing a gale. Charles B. Ela, Company C, accidentally shot in thigh, and died soon after amputation.......Ela was the tallest man of Company C, and received his wound at the hand of the shortest man of the company, Leonard M. Eudy. They were just relieved from guard, and in a playful mood Ela took on the point of his bayonet a hollow soup bone that lay there, which Eudy undertook to knock off in a jocular way, when his gun discharged its contents into Ela's thigh, completely shattering the bones. Eudy was called the 'bantam'; he afterwards became a physician, and died of small pox, November 29, 1876, at Bartlett, N. H., which disease he contracted in New Hampshire from a patient whom he was treating. He was a mere schoolboy at the time of this sad accident, and his sensitive nature was so deeply shocked that he never recovered from its effects."

Private Leonard M. Eudy, Company "C," 15th New Hampshire Volunteers

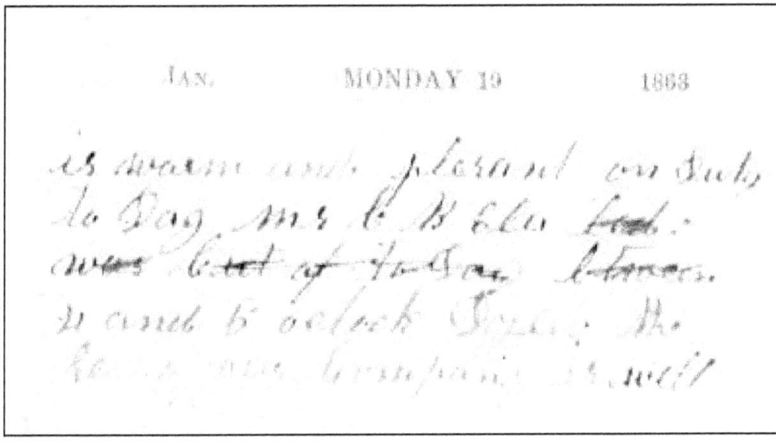
JAN. MONDAY 19 1863

January 19, 1863 – is warm and plesant on Duty to Day mr. C. B. Ela died between 4 and 5 o'clock the rest of our Company is well.

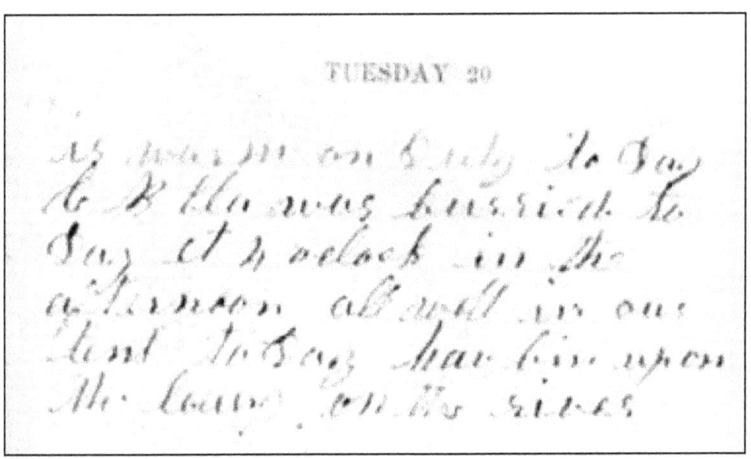
TUESDAY 20

January 20, 1863 – is warm on Duty to Day C. B. Ela was burried today at 4 o'clock in the afternoon all well in our tent to Day hav bin upon the levy on the river.

Charles B. Ela was from Bath and enlisted as a private at age 32 and mustered into Company "C," 15th New Hampshire Volunteers on October 8, 1862. His records indicate that he died of injuries on January 19, 1863 at Carrollton, Louisiana, as described earlier.

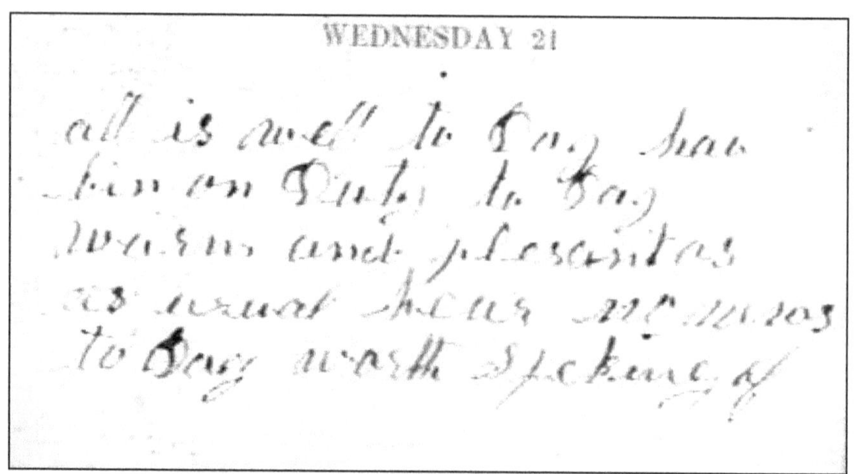

WEDNESDAY 21

January 21, 1863 – all is well to Day hav bin on Duty to Day warm and plesant as usual hear no news to Day worth speking of.

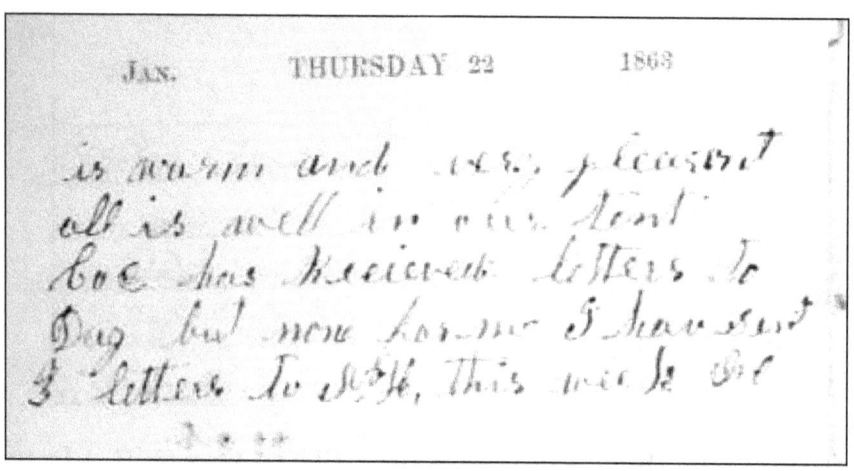

JAN. THURSDAY 22 1863

January 22, 1863 – is warm and very pleasant all is well in our tent Co E has Recieved letters to Day but none for us I have sent 3 letters to NH this week.

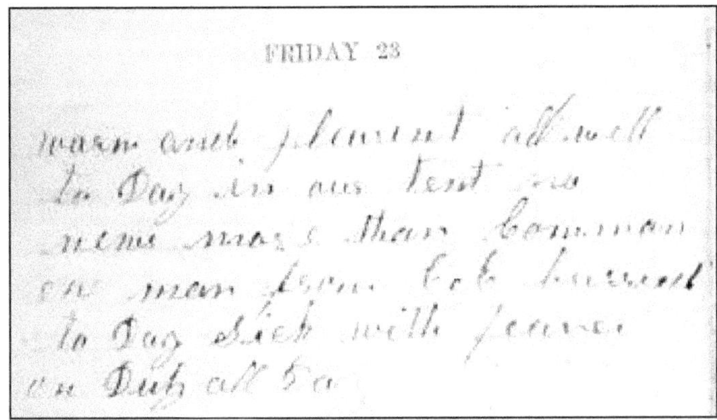
FRIDAY 23

January 23, 1863 – warm and pleasant all well to Day in our tent no news more than Common one man from Co E buried to Day Sick with feaver on Duty all Day.

McGregor recalls: "While the regiment was on the march, William H. Hodgman, Company E., died at Camp Mansfield, and was buried without the usual military honors, probably because his disease was malignant; he was delirious."

William H. Hodgman was from Bedford, New Hampshire and was eighteen years old when he enlisted as a private on September 23, 1862. On October 15, 1862 he was mustered into Company "E" – New Hampshire 15th Infantry.

SATURDAY 24

January 24, 1863 – warm and pleasant all well in our tent big Steemer landed in Carrollton to Day on Duty all Day no newes to mention.

JAN. SUNDAY 25 1863

is warm and pleasant all is well in our tent no news of eny importence to Day evry thing goes loveley with us now house and out bildings Burnt to Day in Carrollton

January 25, 1863 – is warm and pleasant all is well in our tent no news of eny importence to Day every thing goes loveley with us now house and out bildings Burnt to Day in Carrollton.

McGregor recalls: "Fire in Carrollton to-night – house and other buildings burned close to our camp; the guard fired to give the alarm."

MONDAY 26

is Rather Cool to Day white frost last night Cool winds from the ocean all well to Day as usual is but one or 2 in Coe now that is very sick

January 26, 1863 – is rather Cool to Day white frost last night Cool winds from the ocean as well to Day as usual is but one or 2 in Co e now that is very sick.

TUESDAY 27

rather rainey to Day hav
written 2 letters to Day
and sent them off one to
Charles H Foster of Lowell
Mass one to Curtis Foster
of Littleton N.H.

January 27, 1863 – rather rainey to Day hav written 2 letters to Day and sent them off one to Charles H Foster of Lowell Mass one to Curtis Foster of Littleton NH.

On the 27th of January, orders were received to move up the river to Camp Parapet.

On the 28th McGregor recalls: "January 28, Wednesday. Cold morning; very pleasant. Struck tents at 8 A.M., and marched in mud four inches deep, to the parapet and encamped on same ground that had been occupied by the Sixteenth New Hampshire; very hard day's work......The Sixteenth had just vacated the ground on which we encamped, and left cook houses standing, which were utilized by us; our cooking had previously been done in the open air."

The "luxury"of a cook house.

In the field, and in most camps, cooking was done out of doors and covered "cook houses" were infrequent.

Open Air Cooking

Camp Parapet was located north of Carrollton and the fortifications were designed by Major General David E. Twiggs, commanding Confederate Department Number One. The plan called for a breastwork that would essentially protect the city of New Orleans from an attack from Union forces coming down the river from the north. The fort stretched from the river on the west to a swamp on the right, a distance of about a mile. The New Orleans Daily Picayune described the fort as having a parapet nine feet high, with a moat thirty feet wide and six feet deep in the front.

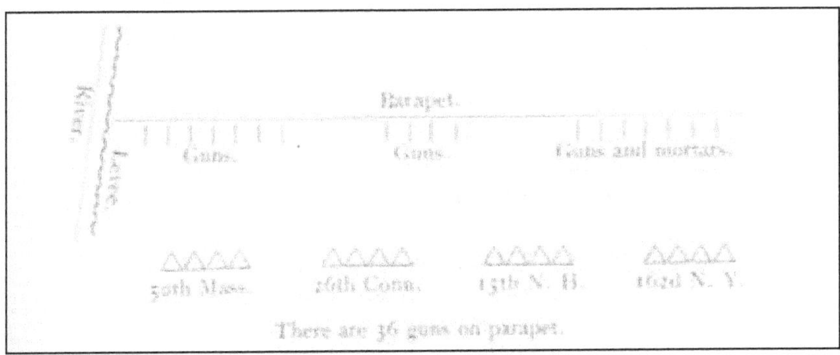

McGregor's Sketch of the Gun Emplacements at Camp Parapet

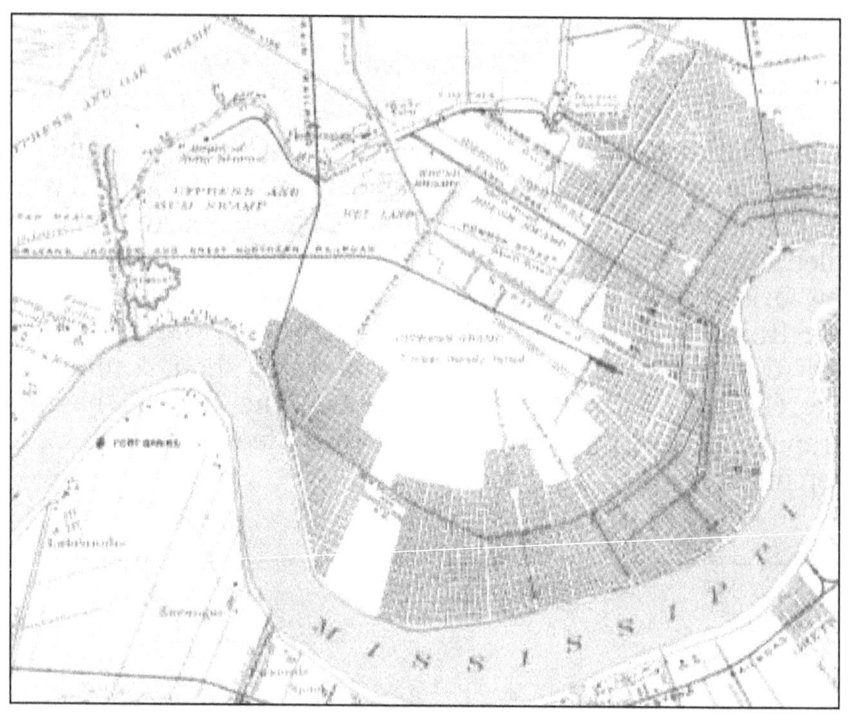

Location of Camp Parapet (left center) from a survey entitled:

**"APPROACHES TO NEW ORLEANS – Prepared by order of Maj. Gen. N. P. Banks
Feb. 14, 1863"
(Author's collection)**

Sadly, very little remains of Camp Parapet today – the photographs on the following page were taken by the author during a visit to Carrollton in 2009.

CAMP PARAPET
In 1862 Confederate and Louisiana authorities laid out Camp Parapet as a part of the defense lines of New Orleans. The works were designed to protect the city against an attack from the north. After the Federals coming up from the south, captured New Orleans, Camp Parapet became an important part of the Union defenses. It served also as a training camp for Northern soldiers.

CAMP PARAPET
REMAINS OF
OLD POWDER MAGAZINE

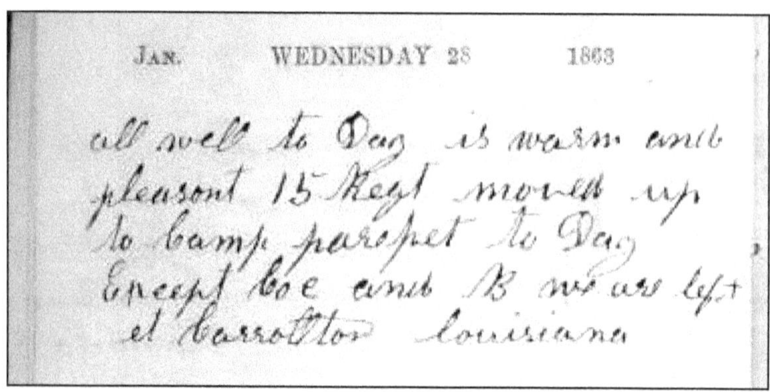

JAN. WEDNESDAY 28 1863

all well to Day is warm and
pleasont 15 Regt moved up
to Camp parapet to Day
Except Co C and B we are left
et Carrollton louisiana

January 28, 1863 – all well to Day is warm and pleasant 15 Regt moved up to Camp parapet to Day Except Co C and B we are left et Carrollton louisiana.

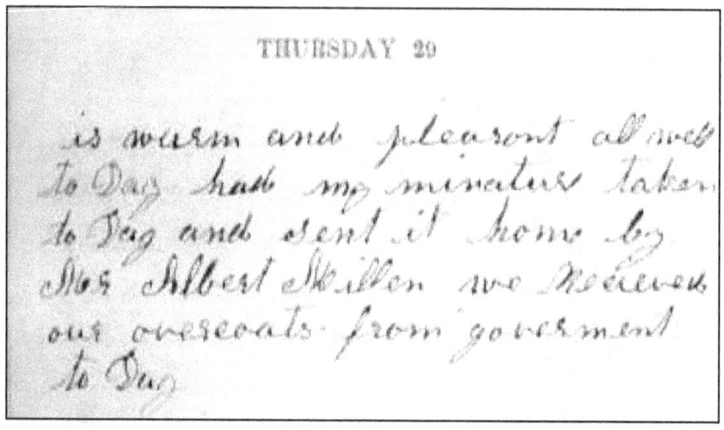

THURSDAY 29

is warm and pleasont all well
To Day had my minature taken
to Day and sent it home by
Mr Albert Millen we Recieved
our overcoats from goverment
to Day

January 29, 1863 – is warm and pleasant all well to Day had my minature taken to Day and sent it home by Mr Albert Millen we Recieved our overcoats from goverment to Day.

Albert Millen was from Lyman and enlisted at age 42 as a private, on December 20, 1861 he was mustered into Company "H" of the 8th Regiment New Hampshire Volunteers – he was discharged for disability on December 5, 1862 at Camp Stevens, Louisiana.

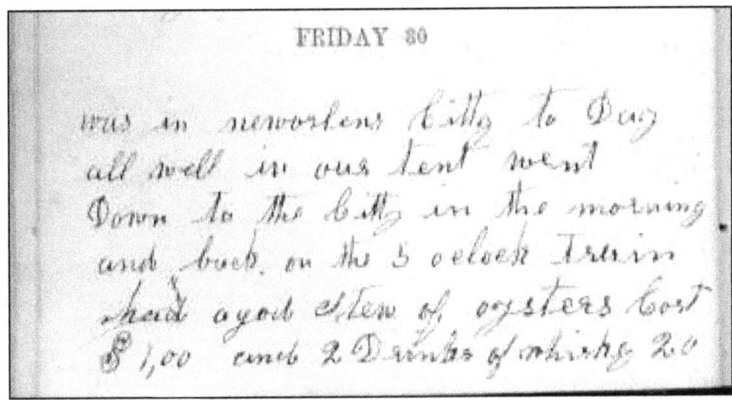

FRIDAY 30

was in neworlens Citty to Day all well in our tent went Down to the Citty in the morning and back on the 5 oclock Train had a good Stew of oysters Cost $1,00 and 2 Drinks of whisky 20

January 30, 1863 – was in new Orleans Citty to Day all well in our tent went Down to the Citty in the morning and back on the 5 o clock Train had a good stew of oysters Cost $1.00 and 2 Drinks of whisky.

JAN. SATURDAY 31 1863

is very warm and plesont one man from Mass Regt Burried to Day all well in our Tent har bin upp on the Shell road to Drum the guards upp and back to Discharg thire guns

January 31, 1863 – is very warm and plesant one man from Mass Regt Burried to Day all well in our tent here bin up on the Shell road to drum the guards up and back to Discharge thire guns.

Chapter Two
February, 1863

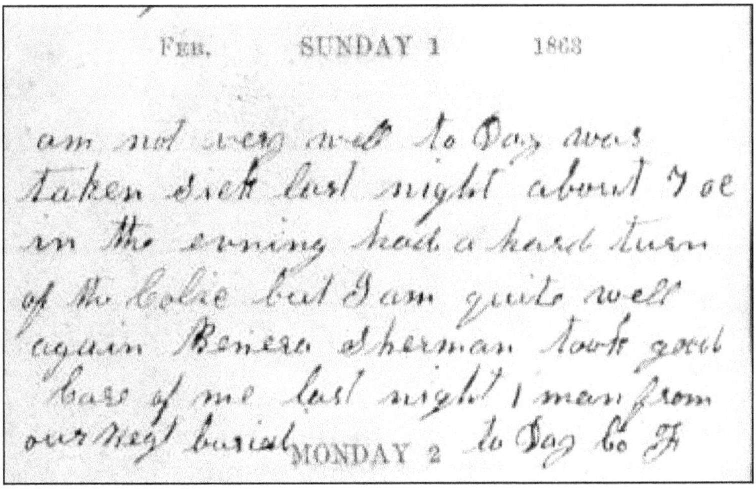
FEB. SUNDAY 1 1863

am not very well to Day was
taken sick last night about 7 oc
in the evening had a hard turn
of the Colic but I am quite well
again Benera Sherman took good
care of me last night 1 man from
our Regt buried MONDAY 2 to Day Co F

February 1, 1863 - am not very well to day was taken sick last night about 7 o'c in the evening had a hard turn of the Colic but I am quite well again Benera Sherman took good care of me last night 1 man from our Regt buried to day Co F.

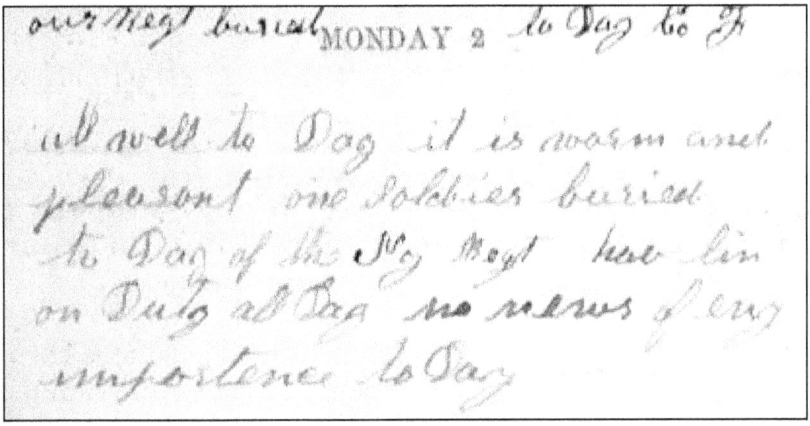
our Regt buried MONDAY 2 to Day Co F

all well to Day it is warm and
pleasant one Soldier buried
to Day of the NY Regt have bin
on Duty all Day no news of eny
importence to Day

February 2, 1863 – all well to Day it is warm and pleasant on Soldier buried to Day of the NY Regt hav bin on Duty all Day no news of eny importence to Day.

FEB. TUESDAY 3 1863

all well to Day it is hot hear
one man buried from our Regt
to Day no leters from home
Some for the Company but non
for me

February 3, 1863 – all well to Day it is hot hear one man buried from our Regt to Day no leters from home Some for the Company but none for me.

WEDNESDAY 4

Rather cool to Day thunderd and
litened and rained hard last
night one man buried from
our Regt to Day Colby from
Co F

February 4, 1863 – Rather cool to day thunderd and litened and rained hard last night - one man buried from our Regt. to day Colby from Company "F".

George F. Colby was from Springfield and enlisted as a corporal at age 18 and mustered into Company "F," 15th New Hampshire Volunteers on October 10, 1862. His records indicate that he died of disease on February 2, 1863 at Carrollton, Louisiana.

McGregor recalls that Colby died on the 2nd: ".....George F. Colby, Company F, died to-day at Carrollton". An earlier notation of the death reads as follows: "George F. Colby, age 18, of brain fever, at Carrollton, La., Monday, February 2, 1863. Chalmette National Cemetery, grave No. 8,155. Disinterred from Carrollton avenue. His headstone is erroneously marked, "Co. C, First N. H. Cavalry."

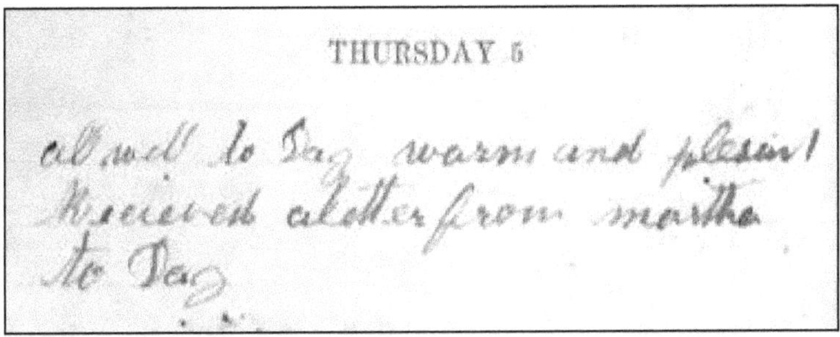

THURSDAY 5

all well to Day warm and plesant
Received a letter from martha
to Day

February 5, 1863 – all well to Day   warm and plesant Received a letter from martha to Day.

Richard refers to Martha several times in his diary and it is not fully known who Martha was. Evidently Richard was married several times, perhaps as many as four, so it is possible that Martha may have been his wife at that time. His first known wife was Susan Mason, the second was Eliza Barrett and the third was Laura Whipple. Richard and Susan had two sons; Eliza bore a daughter, probably Susan Dodge Dexter. In one section of the diary Richard writes about Martha having left bed and board having brought disgrace on her name.

FEB. FRIDAY 6 1863

well all Day writing letters to
Day no news of importence
out on provost guard braut
in 3 prisoners one sargent
help Isaac Smith Catch a nother
man in the nite

February 6, 1863 – well all Day writing letters to Day no news of importence out on provost guard braut in 3 prisoners one sergeant – helped Isaac Smith catch another man in the nite.

SATURDAY 7

all well to Day Sent 3 letters home 1 to martha 1 to albert and marey 1 to amos Smith and 1 to Lowell to horas Smith

February 7, 1863 – all well to Day Sent 3 letters home 1 to Martha 1 to albert and marey 1 to amos Smith and 1 to Lowell to horas Smith.

SUNDAY 8

all is well to Day in our tent I Smith is not very well I went out on petrole guard took in 15 prissorners one Sargent one Carporel

February 8, 1863 – all is well to Day in our tent I Smith is not very well I went out on petrole guard took in 15 prissorners one Sargent and one Corporel.

Mc Gregor notes: "We are now permanently brigaded under General Dow, with the Sixth Michigan, One Hundred and Twenty-eighth New York, and the Twenty-sixth Connecticut, and are encamped as by the following diagram:"

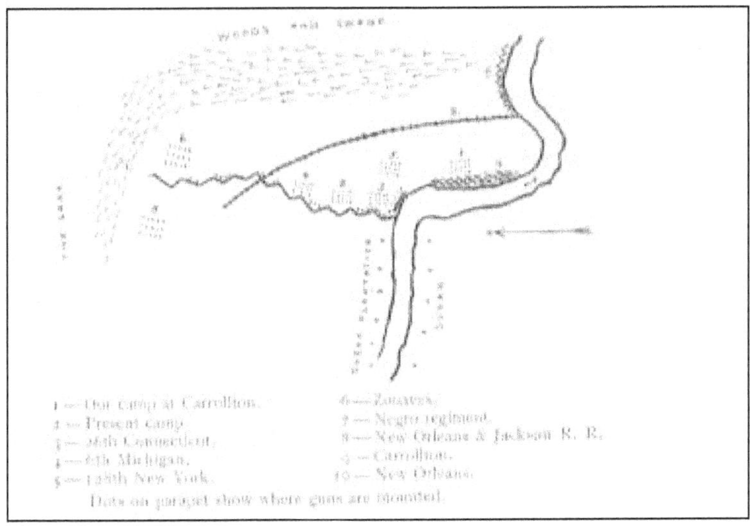

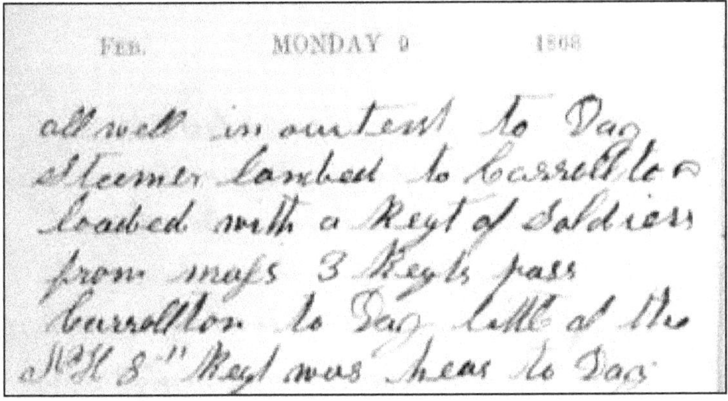

FEB. MONDAY 9 1863

all well in our tent to Day
Steemer landed to Carrollton
loaded with a Regt of Soldiers
from mass 3 Regts pass
Carrollton to Day little at the
NH 8th Regt was hear to Day

February 9, 1863 – all well in our tent to Day Steemer landed to Carrollton loaded with a Regt of Soldiers from mass 3 Regt pass Carrollton to Day.

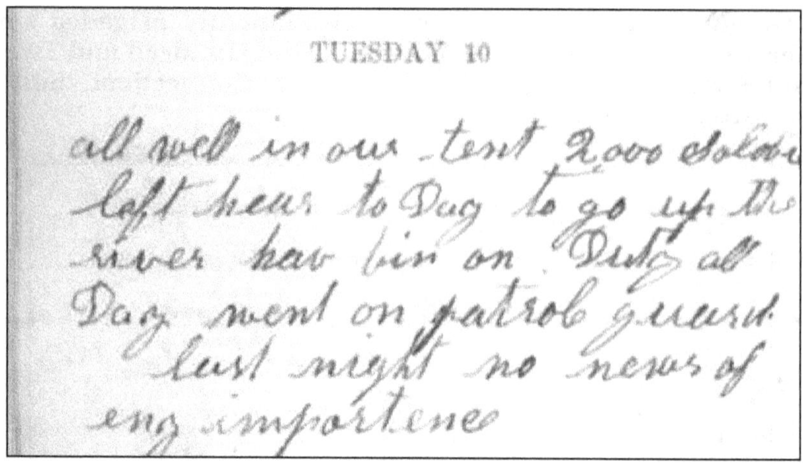
TUESDAY 10

all well in our tent 2000 Soldi[ers]
left hear to Day to go up the
river hav bin on Duty all
Day went on patrole guard
last night no news of
eny importence

February 10, 1863 – all well in our tent 2,000 Soldiers left hear to Dya to go up the river hav bin on Duty all Day went on patrole guard last night no news of eny importence.

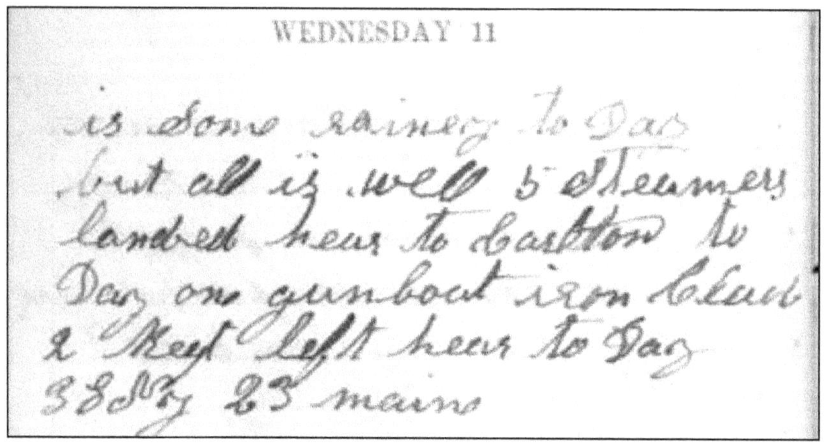
WEDNESDAY 11

is Some rainey to Day
but all is well 5 Steamers
landed hear to Carlton to
Day one gunboat iron Clad
2 Regt left hear to Day
38 NY 23 maine

February 11, 1863 – is Some rainey to Day but all is well 5 Steamers landed here to Carlton to Day one gunboat iron Clad 2 Regt left hear to Day 38 NY 23 maine.

FEB. THURSDAY 12 1863

all well and plesant to Day
one Shipp landed hear to Day
the John Pebody with the 4th
Mass 700 Soldiers on board
and has bin 46 Days et
Sea Soldiers in good Condition

February 12, 1863 – all well and plesant to Day one Shipp landed hear to Day the John Pebody with the 4th Mass 700 Soldiers on board and has bin 46 Days et Sea Soldiers in good Condition.

FRIDAY 13

all well and plesant weather
no news of eny importence
onley a row about Cooking
and Co funds Soldiers goin
upp the river pretty fast
evry Day now

February 13, 1863 – all well and plesant weather no news of eny importence onley a row about Cooking and Co funds Soldiers goin upp the river pretty fast evry Day now.

BRINGING IN A PRISONER

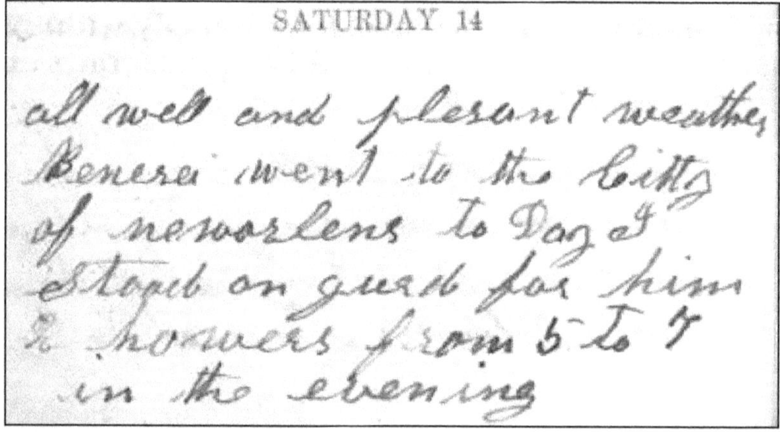

SATURDAY 14

all well and plesant weather
Benera went to the Citty
of neworlens to Day I
Stoped on guard for him
2 howers from 5 to 7
in the evening

February 14, 1863 - all well and pleasant weather Benera Sherman went to the Citty of neworlens to Day I Stood guard for him showers from 5 to 7 in the evening.

The trip into New Orleans was via the Carrollton and New Orleans railway. The railway began service in 1835 and remains in service to this day. Initially, the streetcars were horse drawn, but around the start of the Civil War the railway converted to steam, which proved to be controversial because of the speed and the noise generated by the engines. The New Orleans streetcars remain in service and the car to Carrollton is via the St. Charles Avenue line.

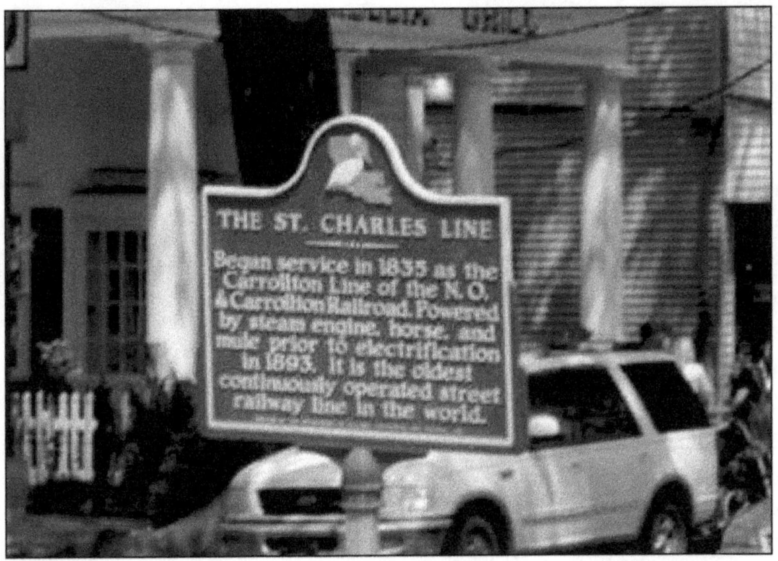

The St. Charles Line – This sign appears on South Carrollton Avenue in Carrollton near where Camp Mansfield was located.
(Photo by the Author)

This photograph was taken from the inside of the St. Charles Line streetcar heading up South Carrollton Avenue in Carrollton. This is the line that Richard, Isaac, Benera and their comrades would have traveled to go into New Orleans.
(Photo by the Author)

February 15, 1863 – ruther Dull and lowery to Day Stood guard all night last night for Benera Sherman. One man jumped out of the hosspitlle window to [two] Storey high was hurt very badly.

February 16, 1863 – all well to Day in our tent 2 soldiers from our Regt Burried to Day we had a very hard thunder Shower last night Sail Ship Herald arrived from Boston in 20 Days loaded with provisions 2 Steamers landed hear to Carlton to Day.

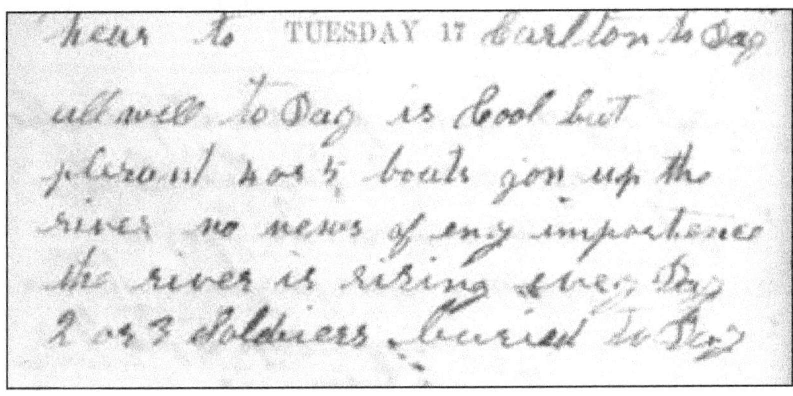

hear to TUESDAY 17 Carlton to Day
all well to Day is Cool but
plesant 4 or 5 boats gon up the
river no news of eny importence
the river is rising every Day
2 or 3 Soldiers buried to Day

February 17, 1863 – all well to Day is Cool but plesant 4 or 5 boats gon up the river no news of eny importence the river is rising every Day 2 or 3 soldiers buried to Day.

McGregor recalls a rather humorous incident: "Lieutenant Durgin was stationed at lower end of the parapet next to the swamp, with thirty of the guard. In undertaking to leap a ditch he fell in, and was completely submerged, creating much merriment among his men."

Woodbury M. Durgin was thirty-seven years old when he enlisted as a Second Lieutenant on September 18, 1862. On the 3rd of November he was commissioned into Company D, 15th New Hampshire Volunteers.

FEB. WEDNESDAY 18 1863

February 18, 1863 – went Down to the Citty of orleans had a good time went to the Cemetery got home Recieved 2 letters from home 1 from Martha.

THURSDAY 19

February 19, 1863 – all well to Day hav bin writing most all Day to Isaac Dodge and one leter to C. Foster 2 of our Soldiers buried to Day one of our Drummers Dead 2 more of them sick

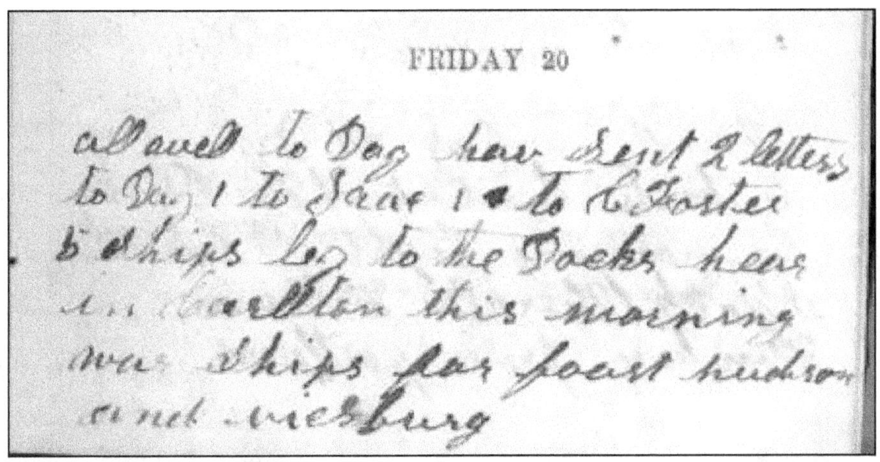

FRIDAY 20

all well to Day hav Sent 2 letters to Day 1 to Isaac 1 to C Foster 5 Ships lay to the Docks hear in Carllton this morning war Ships for foart hudson and vicksburg

February 20, 1863 – all well to Day hav Sent 2 letters to Day 1 to Isaac 1 to C. Foster 5 Ships lay to the Docks hear in Carllton this morning war Ships for foart Hudson and vicksburg.

FEB. SATURDAY 21 1863

all well no news of eny importe on Dutey all Day hav Sent one letter to Issac

February 21, 1863 – all well no news of eny importence on Dutey all Day hav sent one letter to Issac.

McGregor recalls: "In the afternoon, the wind blowing over a stack of guns in the One Hundred and Sixty-fifth (Zouave) New York regiment away to our right, discharged a piece, fatally piercing the body of one of their men and the hand of another."

Group photograph illustrating stacked muskets.

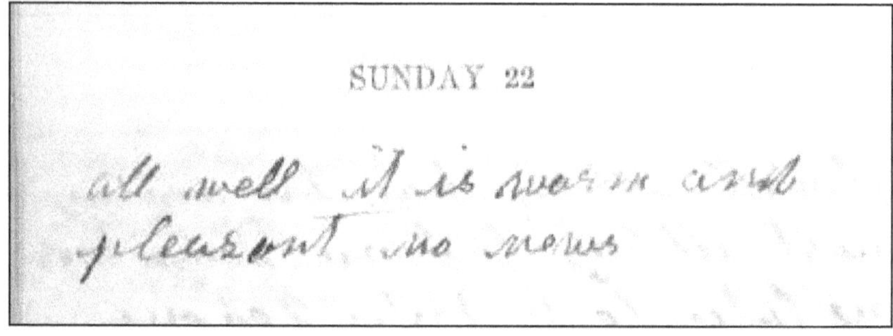

SUNDAY 22

all well it is warm and pleasant no news

February 22, 1863 – all well it is warm and pleasant no news.

It was Washington's birthday, evidently Richard was not among those who celebrated.

McGregor recalls: "Sunday. Cool and pleasant. Captain Johnson inspects Company D. Washington's birthday fittingly celebrated; flags float from every mast. The "Portsmouth" fires twenty-one guns at noon; the band saluted. Harrison Messer, Company B, detailed on extra duty at quartermaster's department. Band played several national airs. Perkins, Company H, lieutenant of the guard."

Sloop-of-War U.S.S. Portsmouth Firing a Salute
Looking Northwest from Camp Parapet

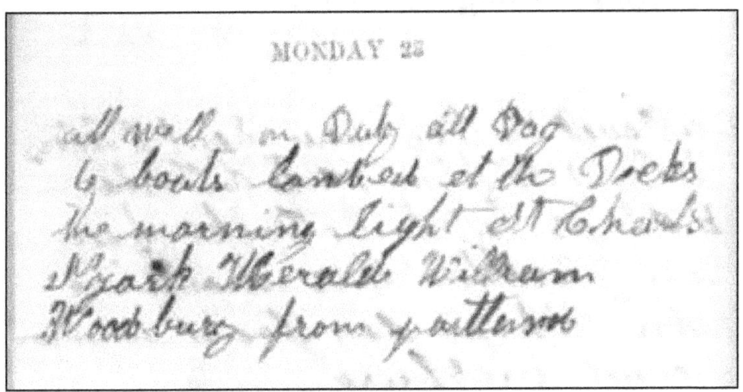

MONDAY 23

all well on Duty all Day
6 boats landed et the Docks
the morning light St Charles
York Herald William
Woodbury from patterson

February 23, 1863 – all well on Duty all Day 6 boats landed et the Docks the morning light St Charles York Herald William Woodbury from patterson

Richard and McGregor were both at Camp Parapet yet Richard evidently didn't see the display of flowers, flags, Chinese lanterns and pyrotechnics from New York that McGregor described. It was reported as a magnificent spectacle and there was music and dancing and a large group from New Orleans in attendance.

FEB. TUESDAY 24 1863

February 24, 1863 – all well and is warm and plesant went to the Citty to Day bought a fiddle and trunk paid 15.00 Came back on the 8 o clock 2 Soldiers buried to Day one from our Regt one from NY Regt.

WEDNESDAY 25

February 25, 1863 – all well hav put in 2 Drum heads for the major hav bin fiddling to Day on my new fiddle it is warm and plesant 2 Soldiers buried to Day Mail Steamer left N.orleans.

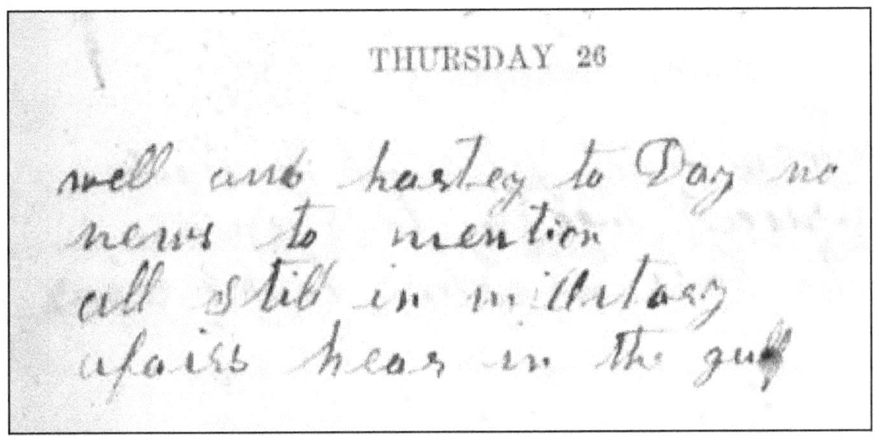

THURSDAY 26

well and hartey to Day no
news to mention
all Still in millitary
afairs hear in the gulf

February 26, 1863 – well and hartey to Day no news to mention all Still in military affairs hear in the gulf.

FEB. FRIDAY 27 1863

all well to Day no news
hav bin fiddling Some
Some Soldiers buried to Day
1 or 2

February 27, 1863 – all well to Day no news hav bin fiddling Some Some Soldiers buried to Day 1 or 2

SATURDAY 28

February 28, 1863 – all well warm and plesant we take Some prisoners   as usual we have taken 4 to Day had a hard fight on levy Street with Some Soldiers.

Chapter Three
March, 1863

MARCH SUNDAY 1 1863

warm and plerant well as
usual begin to run on
the Cars to Day to N orlens

March 1, 1863 – warm and plesant well as usual begin to run on the Cars to Day to N orlens.

MARCH MONDAY 2 1863

all well hav bin on the Cars
all Day go on et 7 in the
morning and off et half
past 8 o clock in the Evning

March 2, 1863 – all well hav bin on the Cars all Day go on et 7 in the morning and off et half past 8 o clock in the Evning.

TUESDAY 3

all well had our ambrotipes
taken all of the Company to
geather to Day hav bin on
the Cars all Day went Down
on St Charles Street to a bowling
Saloon lieutenant Sargent and myself

March 3, 1863 – all well had our ambrotipes taken all of the Company to geather to Day hav bin on the Cars all Day went Down on St Charles Street to a bowling Saloon lieutenant Sargent and myself.

Ambrotypes were essentially photographs that created a positive image on glass but using a collodion process. Although the wet plate process was invented by Frederick Scott Archer, James Ambrose Cutting took out a number of patents around 1854 and it is possible that the word "Ambrotype" is based upon his middle name.

THE BOY HAS HIS PICTURE TAKEN.

The method became quite popular because the image was positive as opposed to the negative image created in daguerreotypes, also ambrotypes were less expensive and many were tinted by hand.

Subjects were required to hold their pose from anywhere between five to sixty or more seconds, depending on the availability and quality of light. Because they were somewhat fragile, Ambrotypes were often contained in folding cases. Unfortunately, Richard's Ambrotype was destroyed years ago and no longer exists.

Example of a Cased Ambrotype
(Author's collection)

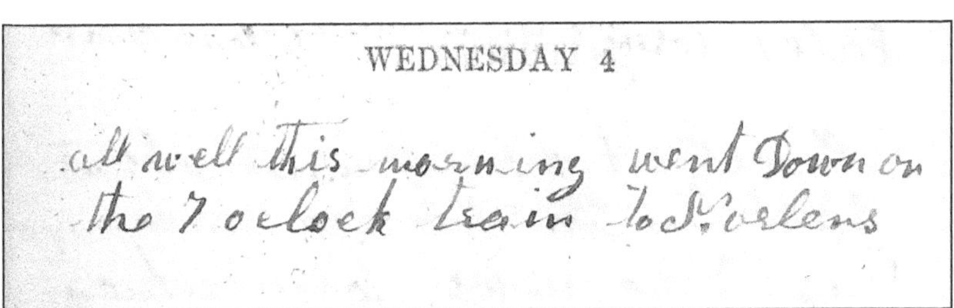

WEDNESDAY 4

all well this morning went Down on
the 7 oclock train to N orlens

March 4, 1863 – all well this morning went Down on the 7 o clock train to N orlens.

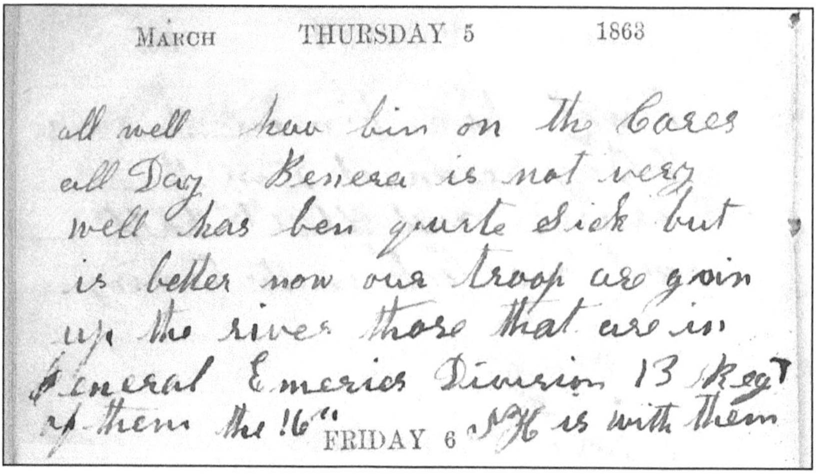

March 5, 1863 – all well have bin on the Cares all Day. Benera is not very well has been quite Sick but is better now our troops are goin up the river those that are in General Emeries* Division 13 Regt. of the them 16th NH is with them.

McGregor's notes read in part: "Orders read to provide ourselves with one hundred rounds ammunition and be ready to move at a moment's notice."

William H. Emory Commanded the Nine-

*General William H. Emory was born on September 7, 1811 and was graduated from the United States Military Academy in 1831, he ranked fourteenth out of a class of thirty-three. In March, 1863 he was attached to the Army of the Gulf.

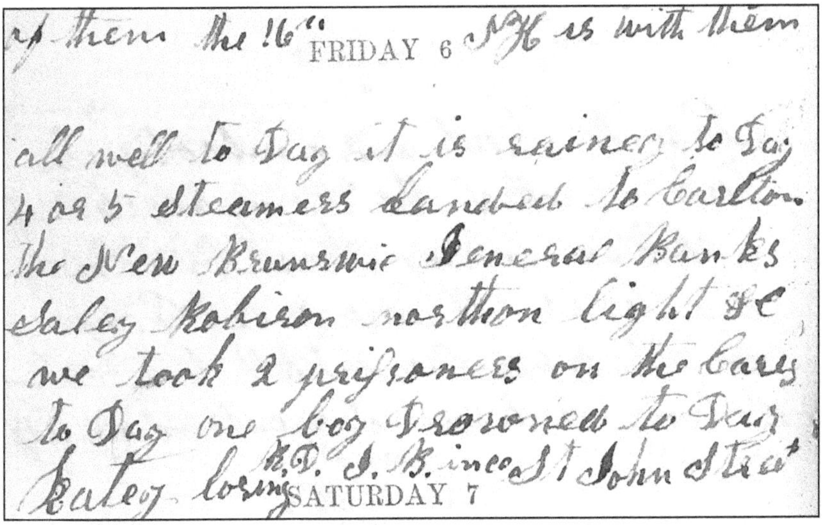
of them the 16th FRIDAY 6 NH is with them

all well to Day it is rainey to Day
4 or 5 Steamers landed to Carlton
the New Brunswic General Banks
Saley Robison northon light &c
we took 2 prisoners on the Cares
to Day one boy Drowned to Day
Katey loring R.D. J. B. ince St John Street SATURDAY 7

March 6, 1863 – all well to Day it is rainey to Day 4 or 5 Steamers landed to Carlton the New Brunswick General Banks Saley Robison northern light, [etc.] we took 2 prisoners on the Cares to Day one boy Drowned to Day R.D. ?????????????

McGregor reported that "....under marching orders.......Sixteenth and Eighth New Hampshire went up river.....Gunboats and transports loaded with troops constantly passing up."

The entire time that Richard and his comrades were in the Carrollton area, plans were underway to open up the Mississippi river.

Back in November, Major-General N. P. Banks sailed from New York to New Orleans with a large number of troops. His orders were to relieve General Butler and proceed northward up the Mississippi to join General Grant at Vicksburg, thereby gaining complete control of the Mississippi River pursuant to the so-called Anaconda Plan which will be discussed in more detail later.

Richard and his comrades will not be called into action until later, but signs of the upcoming battle at Port Hudson are beginning to develop.

SATURDAY 7

all well it warm and plesont
hav bin on the train to
Day no news to mention

March 7, 1863 – all well it warm and plesant hav bin on the train to Day no news to mention.

McGregor notes that: "Gunboats and transports loaded with troops go up river all day and all night."

Transports on the Mississippi Awaiting Orders

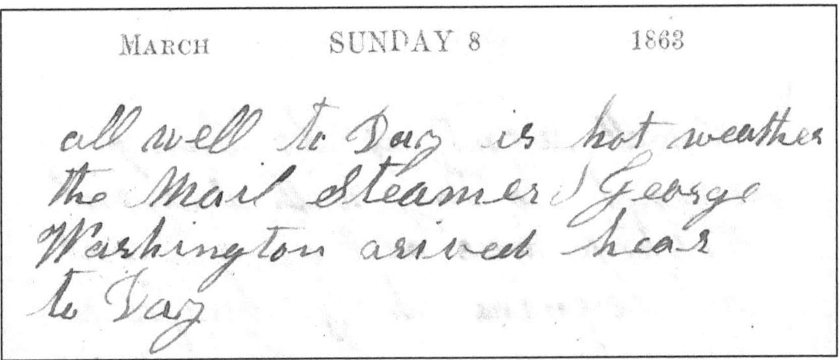

MARCH SUNDAY 8 1863

all well to Day is hot weather the Mail Steamer George Washington arrived hear to Day

March 8, 1863 – all well to Day is hot weather the Mail Steamer George Washington arrived hear to Day.

McGregor recalls: "All troops between us and New Orleans now gone.....Ironclad "Essex" and several other steamers went up river.....Went down to the river and saw the gunboat "Essex" going up."

Ironclad "Essex" – Baton Rouge, Louisiana - 1862

The Ironclad "Essex" was constructed in 1856 as a steam-powered ferry, it was named after Essex, Massachusetts. It's length was 250 feet, beam was sixty feet, draft was six feet and speed was five and one-half knots; crew complement was 124. For armament it carried 1 x 32 pounder, 3 x 11 inch Dahlgren smooth bores, 1 x 10 inch Dahlgren smooth bore and 1 x 12 pounder Howitzer.

MONDAY 9

all well in Camp to Day is
little Cooler to Day I recieved
a letter from Martha to Day
2 large Steamers went up
the river last night

March 9, 1863 – all well in Camp to Day is little Cooler to Day I recieved a letter from Martha to Day 2 large Steamers went up the river last night.

TUESDAY 10

all well to Day the boys are
in good sperits and wish they
wer to home to go to town
meeting to vote I think they
would all vote the Democratic
Ticket if they Could get home

March 10, 1863 – all well to Day the boys are in good sperits and wish they wer to home to go to town meeting to vote   I think they would all vote the Democratic ticket if they Could get home.

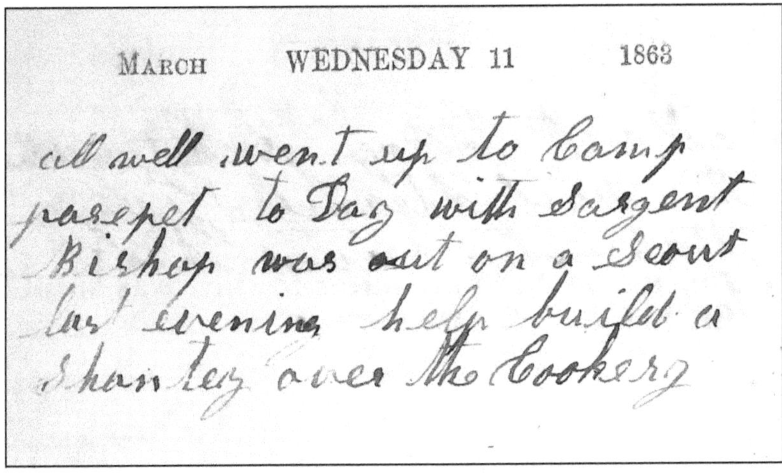

MARCH WEDNESDAY 11 1863

all well went up to Camp
parepet to Day with Sargent
Bishop was out on a Scout
last evening help build a
Shantey over the Cookery

March 11, 1863 - all well went up to Camp Parapet to Day with Sergent Bishop was out on a Scout last evening help build a Shantey over the Cookery.

John Bishop was from Landaff and enlisted as a sergeant at age 44 and mustered into Company "C," 15th New Hampshire Volunteers on October 8, 1862. His records indicate that he died of disease on August 4, 1863 at Memphis, Tennessee.

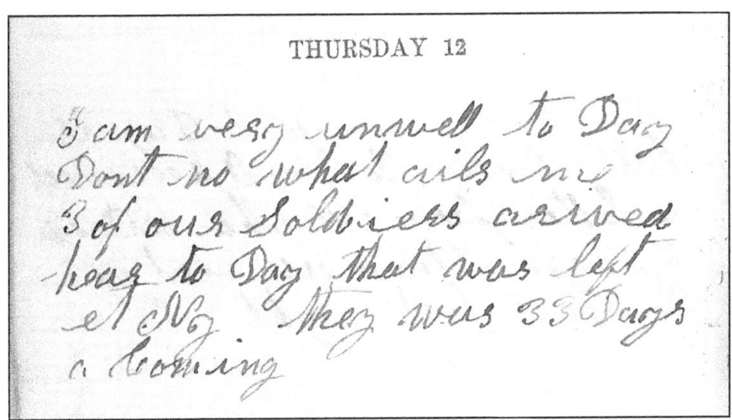

THURSDAY 12

I am very unwell to Day
Dont no what ails me
3 of our Soldiers arrived
hear to Day that was left
et NY they was 33 Days
a Coming

March 12, 1863 – I am very unwell to Day Don't know what ails me 3 of our Soldiers arrived hear to Day that was left et NY they was 33 days a Coming.

FRIDAY 13

I am no better to Day
was auful Sick Last
night hav had the Doctor.

March 13, 1863 – I am no better to Day was auful Sick last night have had the Doctor.

MARCH SATURDAY 14 1863

Dont get eny better yet
hav had the Doctor to Day
my fare is very hard
in Camp

March 14, 1863 – Don't get eny better yet hav had the Doctor to Day my fare is very hard in Camp.

SUNDAY 15

not So well to Day hav
gon to a privat house
was treated kindly by
them the maid got me hot Sling
and got me warm watter to Soak my
feet in on her own accord and
giv me a good Swet

March 15, 1863 – not So well to Day hav gon to a privat house   was treated kindly by them the maid got me hot Sling and got me warm water to Soak my feet in on her own accord and giv me a good Swet.

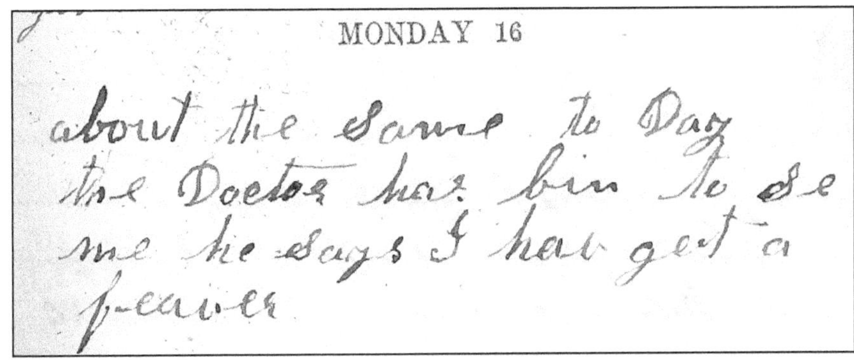

MONDAY 16

about the Same to Day
the Doctor has bin to Se
me he Says I hav get a
feaver

March 16, 1863 – about the Same to Day the Doctor has bin to Se me he Says I hav get a feaver.

MARCH TUESDAY 17 1863

I think I am a little better to
Day hope I Shal get well
again So I Can go home to
my Dear friends I am getting
very weak now I Can hardly
write Benera Staid with me
last night

WEDNESDAY 18

March 17, 1863 – I think I am a little better to Day hope I Shal get well again So I Can go home to my Dear friends I am getting very weak now I Can hardly write Benera Staid with me last night.

last night WEDNESDAY 18

Some better to Day I feel quite Smart and am in better Sperits the Doctor has bin to Se me this Evning and a number of the Boys has bin in to Se me to

March 18, 1863 – Some better to Day I feel quite Smart and am in better Sperits the Doctor has bin in to se me this Evning and a number of the Boys has in to Se me to.

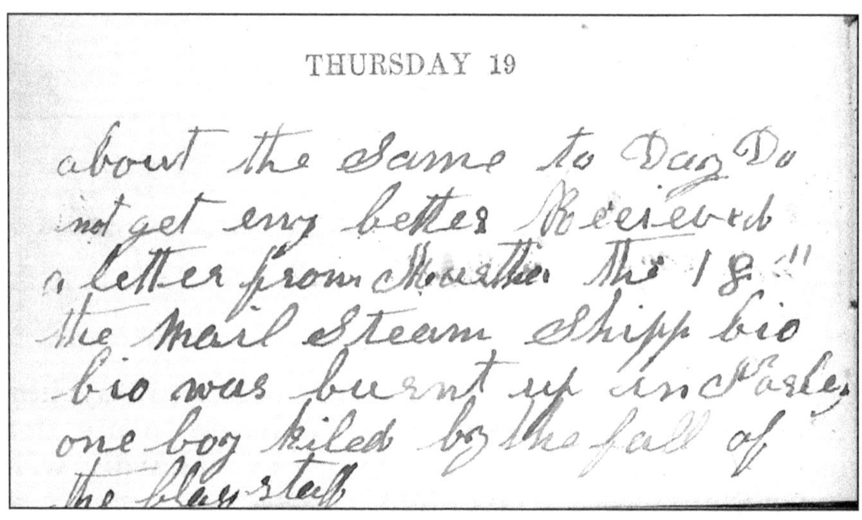

THURSDAY 19

about the Same to Day Do not get eny better Recieved a letter from Martha the 18th the Mail Steam Shipp bio bio was burnt up in N orleans one boy kiled by the fall of the flagstaff

March 19, 1863 – about the Same to Day Do not get eny better Recieved a letter from Martha the 18th the Mail Steam Shipp Bio Bio was burnt up in N orlens one boy killed by the fall of the flagstaff.

MARCH FRIDAY 20 1863

no better to Day Cant Seam
to get help no news is warm
and plesant time Seames
long now

March 20, 1863 – no better to Day Cant Seam to get help no news is warm and plesant time Seames long now.

SATURDAY 21

little letter to Day hav bin
up to the tents is very warm
to Day the Soldiers begin to
talk when they Shal Start
to go home they are ancious to
hav the tim Come

March 21, 1863 – little better to Day hav bin up to the tents is very warm to Day the Soldiers begin to talk when they Shal Start to go home they are ancious to have the time Come.

SUNDAY 22

not So well to Day. Dont hav-
eny apeatite to eat eny thing
no news to mention

March 22, 1863 – not So well to Day   Don't hav eny apetite to eat eny thing no news to mention.

McGregor recalls: "Company D boys shot and brought into camp from the picket line an alligator seven feet long. Some of the flesh was cooked; it was very white and nice looking. But was coarse-grained and had a fishy taste. The lower jaw bone was boiled clean of the flesh and showed a wonderful set of teeth.......Mosquitoes begin their ravages."

MARCH MONDAY 23 1863

Some better to Day have bin taking a good Dose of Caster oil it is rainey to Day and it makes evry thing Dull and very muddey

TUESDAY 24

Some better to Day is rather Cool and windy no news to mention

WEDNESDAY 25

Still on the gain am feeling quite smart no news is warm and plesant

March 23, 24 and 25 finds Richard a little better in terms of his health but reports nothing really new happening in camp.

McGregor pretty much reflected Richard's reports - The weather though was heavy rain, thunder and lightning on the 23rd and showery with hail on the 24th – no drill or parade because of the mud. On the 25th, parades commence, evidently the mud had begun to dry.

MARCH THURSDAY 26 1863

am better to Day hav bin
up to Camp to Day has
bin a little fight up to lake
poncheytrain took 12 prisoners
Som Cotton 2 Ships loads and
lotts of guns and amunition

March 26, 1863 – am better to Day hav bin up to Camp to Day has bin a little fight up to lake poncheytrain took 12 prisoners Some Cotton 2 Ships loads and lots of guns and amunition.

FRIDAY 27

all well to Day no news of
much importence six of our
men was braught in
to the horspittle they wer
wounded in the fight up to
the lake no one killed

SATURDAY 28

all well no news to mention
is warm and plesant
no mail this week
shal look for aletter evry
Day now

Not much happening on the 27th or 28th but Richard appears to be feeling better with each passing day.

MARCH SUNDAY 29 1863

all well is very warm
no news to mention
all Still in the millitary
line

MONDAY 30

all well is a little Cooler to
Day all quiet and Still no
news to Day

TUESDAY 31

all well is hot to Day
Some talk of goin home in
June next hope we Shal

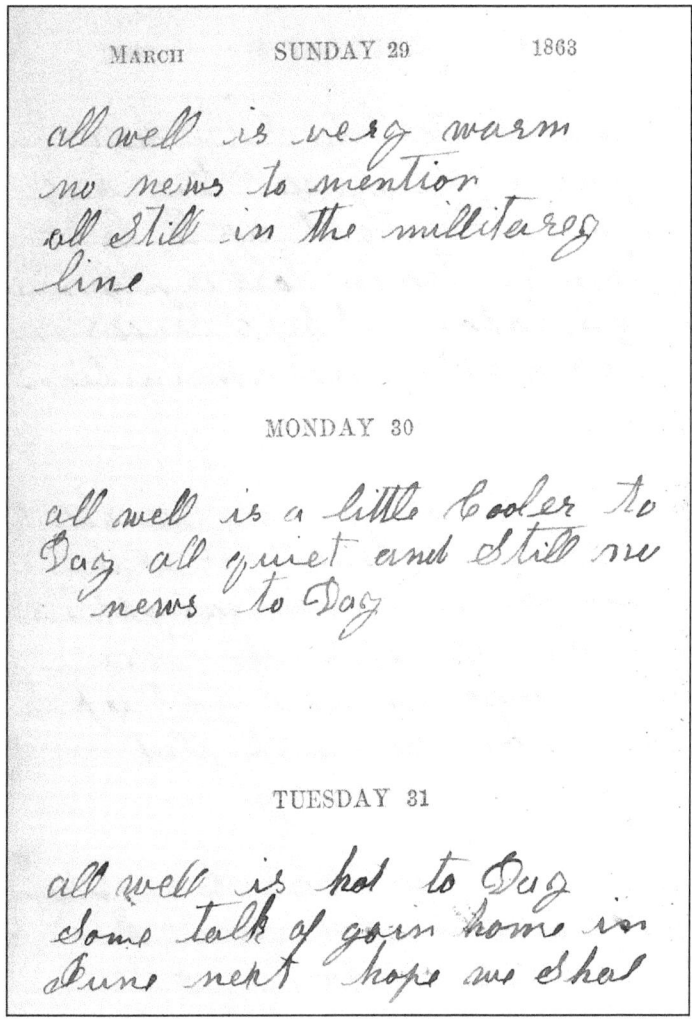

Not much activity as March draws to a close. McGregor reports that the "Portsmouth," while practicing with live shells, sent one wide of the target and exploded over the campsite of the Zouave camp and killed one of their corporals. He further reported that sickness was about the same as the preceding month.

The U.S.S. Portsmouth Firing a Salute
View Looking Northwest from Camp Parapet

Chapter Four
April, 1863

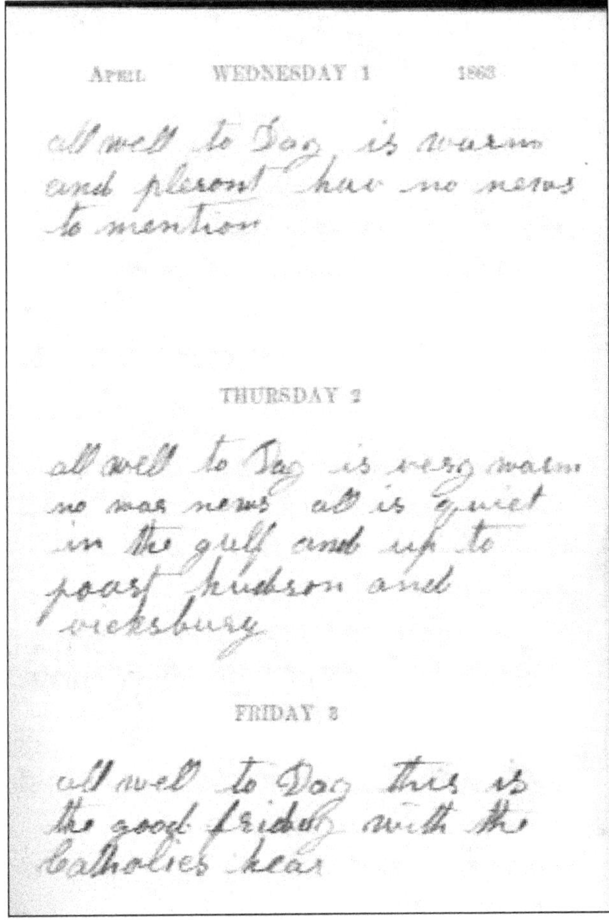

APRIL WEDNESDAY 1 1863

all well to Day is warm and plesont hav no news to mention

THURSDAY 2

all well to Day is very warm no war news all is quiet in the gulf and up to poart hudson and vicksburg

FRIDAY 3

all well to Day this is the good friday with the catholics hear

April 1, 1863 – all well to Day is warm and plesant hav no news to mention

April 2,1863 – all well to Day is very warm no war news all is quiet in the gulf and up to poart Hudson and Vicksburg

April 3, 1863 – all well to Day this is the good Friday with the Catholics hear

It is interesting here that Richard reports that all is quiet in the gulf and up to Port Hudson and Vicksburg, of course he probably wouldn't know that preparations were in progress for the upcoming siege at Port Hudson in May.

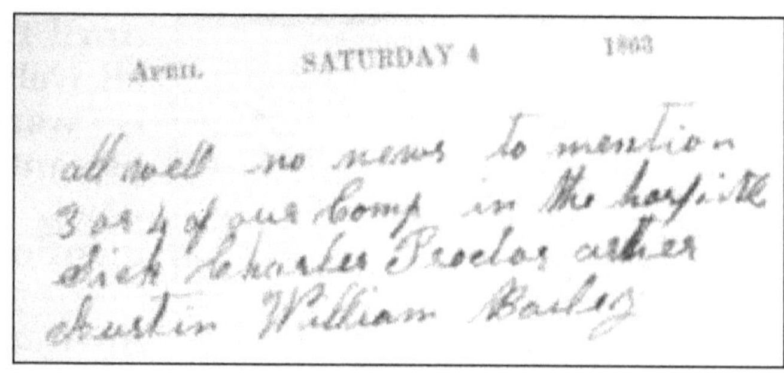

April. SATURDAY 4 1863

all well no news to mention
3 or 4 of our Comp in the hospitl
Sick Charles Proctor arther
Austin William Bailey

April 4, 1863 – all well no news to mention 3 or 4 of our Company in the hospitl Sick Charles Proctor Arther Austin William Bailey.

Charles H. Proctor was from Enfield and enlisted as a private at age 24 and mustered into Company "C," 15th New Hampshire Volunteers on October 8, 1862. He was mustered out on August 13, 1863. No information could be found on William Bailey; the only Baileys that could be found in Company "C" were Benjamin Bailey from Lyman, Henry Bailey from Bath and George W. Bailey from Lyman.

ARTHUR A. AUSTIN—Co. C.

Arthur Austin was also from Enfield and enlisted as a private at age 28 and mustered into Company "C," 15th New Hampshire Volunteers. He was mustered out on August 13, 1863.

An interesting note: Arthur was reported in the regimental hospital at Carrollton on May 20, he became paralyzed and was sent to the hospital at New Orleans. When the regiment arrived in Concord after their tour of duty he was reported dead and preparations made for memorial services. At midnight on the day before the services were to take place he arrived home, evidently very much alive and well.

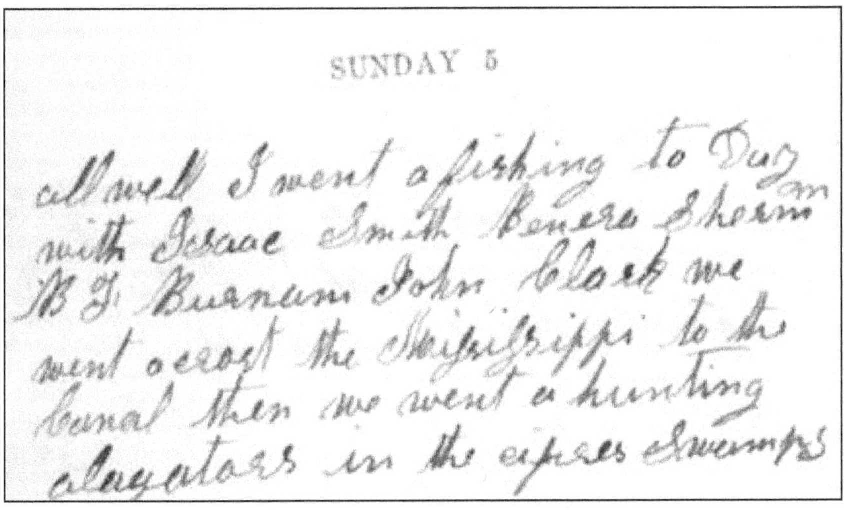

SUNDAY 5

all well I went a fishing to Day
with Isaac Smith Benera Sherman
B F Burnam John Clark we
went accost the Mississippi to the
Canal then we went a hunting
alagatars in the cipres Swamps

April 5, 1863 - all well I went a fishing to day with Isaac Smith, Benera Sherman, B. F. Burnham, John Clarke we went across the Mississippi to the Canal then we went a hunting allagators in the cipres Swamps.

John Clarke was from Bath and enlisted as a private at age 44 and mustered into Company "C," 15th New Hampshire Volunteers on October 8, 1862. His records indicate that he died of disease on August 11, 1863 at Bath, New Hampshire.

BENJAMIN F. BURNHAM—Co. C

Benjamin F. Burnham was from Enfield and enlisted as a Musician at age 36 and mustered into Company "C," 15th New Hampshire Volunteers on September 13, 1862. His records indicate that he died of disease on August 7, 1863 at Chicago, Illinois. Richard's diary notes that he was a "fifer."

Hunting Alligators in the Cypress Swamp

MONDAY 6

all well hav not Dun eny
Dutey Since the furst of
March Dont hav eny Dutey
to Do now

April 6, 1863 – all well hav not Dun eny Dutey Since the furst of March Dont hav eny Dutey to Do now.

APRIL. TUESDAY 7 1863

all well in Camp no news to
mention all is quiet hear
Steam Ship George Washington
from N.Y. arived hear to Day
with U.S. mail

April 7, 1863 – all well in Camp no news to mention all is quiet hear Steam Ship George Washington from NY arived hear to Day with US mail.

WEDNESDAY 8

all well is very hot to Day
Steam Ship pocahontus
arived hear from N.Y. to Day
with mail

April 8, 1863 – all well is very hot to Day Steam Ship pocahontus arived hear from NY to Day with mail

THURSDAY 9

all well is warm and plesant
Recieved a letter from Miss C Foster
of littleton rumers in camp
of goin home in may but I
Dont think we Shal go till june

3

April 9, 1863 – all well is warm and plesant Recieved a letter from Miss C Foster of littleton rumers in camp of goin home in may but I Dont think we Shal go till june.

Three more days with little activity other than ship movement. On the 9th, Richard speaks of rumors in camp about going home- evidently the lack of activity is resulting in boredom and thoughts of leaving for home, however, that will change shortly.

APRIL FRIDAY 10 1863

all well hav ben on a hunting
excursion over the other side of
the Mississippi in the Cypres
Swamps for aligators we got 3 and
Brought 2 of them into Camp one
of them was alive

April 10, 1863 – all well hav ben on a hunting excursion in the Cypres Swamps for aligators we got 3 and Brought 2 of them into Camp one of them was alive.

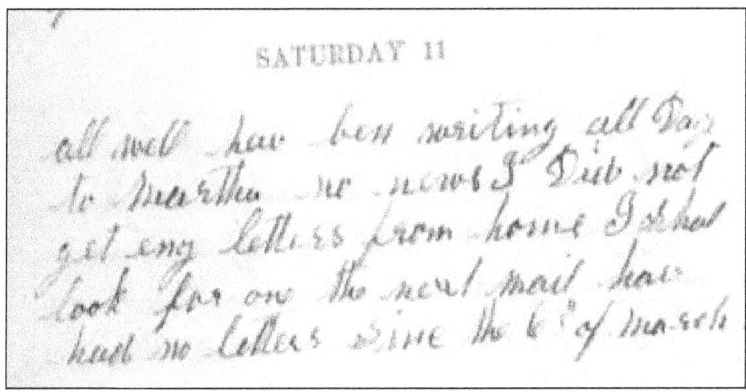

SATURDAY 11

all well hav ben writing all Day to Martha no news I Did not get eny letters from home I Shal look for one the next mail hav had no letters Since the 6th of March

April 11, 1863 – all well hav ben writing all Day to Martha no news. I Did not get eny letters from home I Shal look for one the next mail hav had no letters Since the 6th of March

April 12, 1863 – all well is very warm hav had no raine for a long time hav written a letter to David Dodge and one to C Foster of littleton no news to mention hear.

APRIL MONDAY 13 1863

April 13, 1863 – all well is a little Cooler Some of the Boys has bin a Blackberrien to Day they Did get a lot of them all ripe and Good and very large ones to

Freshly picked blackberries on Monday seemed to have hit the spot for Richard and some of his comrades.

TUESDAY 14

April 14, 1863 – all well the Steam Ship Marion with Mail and 2,000,000 in money for the Soldiers is reported wrecked on florida Reefs neer Kee west the Steam Ship George Washington with mail left for NY to Day.

McGregor recalls: "Mail steamer "Marion" twelve days overdue, and great fear she is lost."

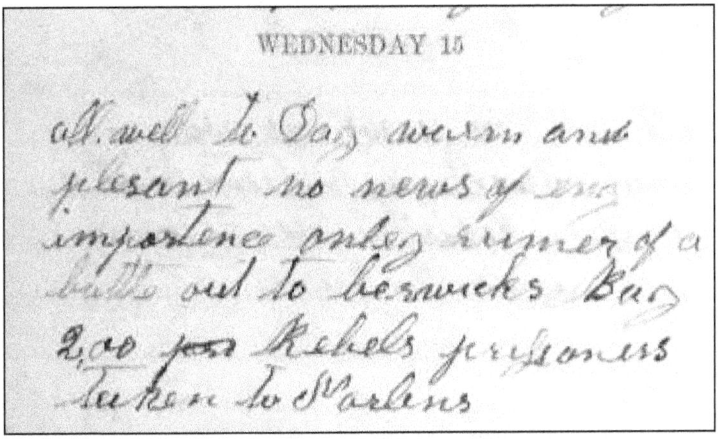

WEDNESDAY 15

all well to Day warm and plesant no news of eny importence onley rumer of a battle out to berwicks Bay 200 Rebels prissoners taken to N orlens

April 15, 1863 – all well to Day warm and plesant no news of eny importence onley rumer of a battle out to berwicks Bay 200 Rebels prissoners taken to N orlens.

McGregor comments: "Rumored that the Sixteenth New Hampshire met the enemy at Berwick Bay, and lost two hundred.........A man attempting to run the guard was shot through the body, and died in ten minutes. He proved to be a citizen, and had apparently been fishing. On being challenged by the guard, he paid no heed. The method of challenge by the guard at the picket line was this: 'Who goes there? Halt – halt – halt!' If at the third call the challenged party does not come to a stand and account for himself, then the guard is to fire. None can cross the line in the daytime without a written pass or in the night without the countersign."

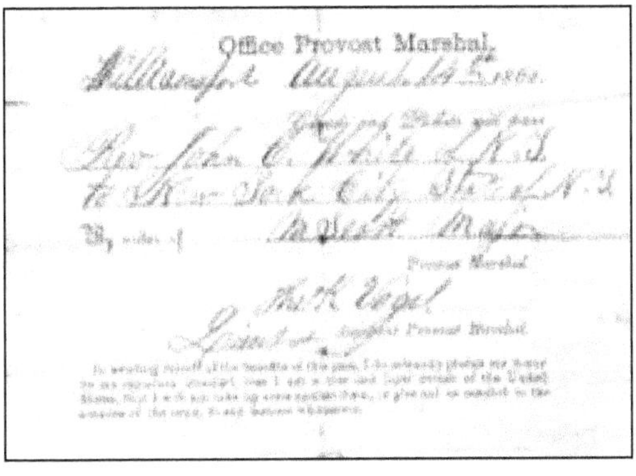

Office Provost Marshal.

Provost Marshal

Typical Pass
(Author's collection)

Challenge at the Picket Line "Who goes there?" – "Friends." – "Dismount, one friend, advance, and give the countersign." Harper's Weekly – February 14, 1863 (Author's collection)

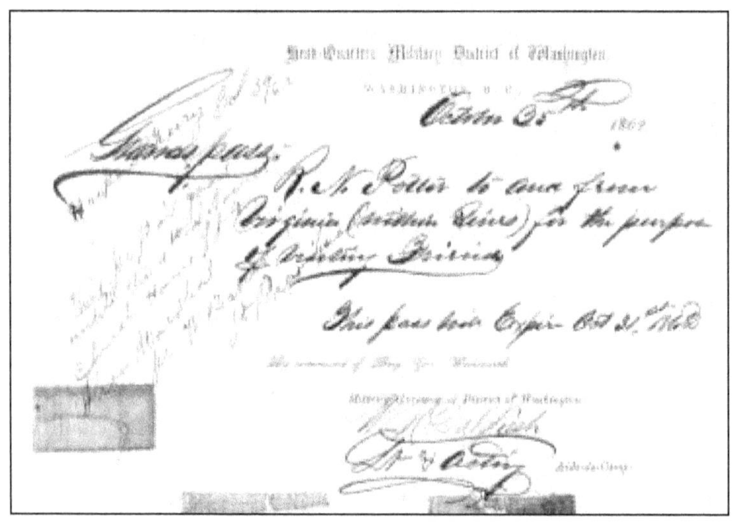

October 25th

R. N. Potter to and from Virginia (within lines) for the purpose of visiting friends

This pass will expire Oct 31st 1862

Another Example of a Pass (Author's collection)

APRIL THURSDAY 16 1863

all well is hot weather to Day
one Rebbel Spye Shot up to
Camp parapet no more news
general neal Dow was in
Camp to Day

April 16, 1863 – all well is hot weather to Day on Rebbel Spye Shot up to Camp parapet no more news general neal Dow was in Camp to Day.

FRIDAY 17

all well in Camp is very
warm one negro Shot hear to
Day one Soldier Shot in orlens
axidentley Steam Ship Creole
arrived to Day with maile
from NY.

April 17, 1863 – all well in Camp is very warm one negro Shot hear to Day on Soldier Shot in orlens axidentley Steam Ship Creole arrived to Day with maile from NY

McGregor notes: "One of a negro regiment was shot last night for running the guard."

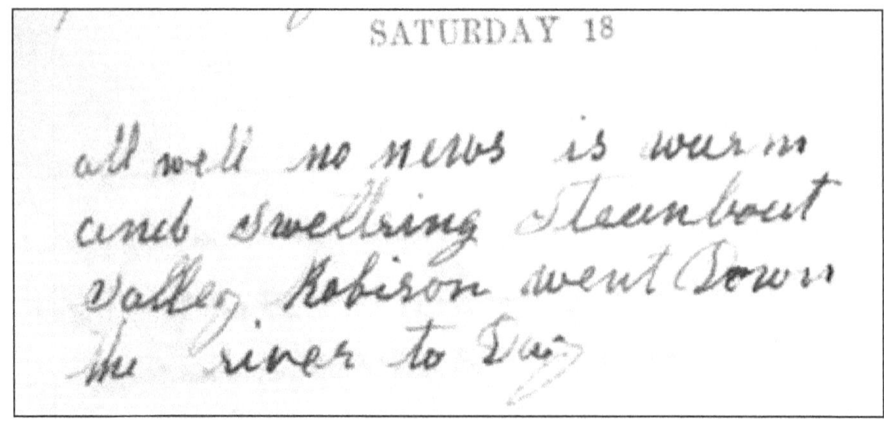

SATURDAY 18

all well no news is warm and Sweltring Steamboat Salley Robison went Down the river to Day

April 18, 1863 – all well no news is warm and Sweltring Steamboat Salley Robison went Down the river to Day.

McGregor writes: "The One Hundred and Twenty-eighth New York left for an excursion across the lakes, Our regiment was designated for this excursion, but the One Hundred and Twenty-eighth was sent instead because so many of our officers were sick. This drew from General Sherman the remark that the Fifteenth New Hampshire was the damnedest regiment for sick officers that he ever saw"

APRIL SUNDAY 19 1863

all well is warm and plesant now 15,00 Rebel prissoners taken By General Banks 2,00 and 50 wounded Soldiers in the hospittle in N orlenes

April 19, 1863 – all well is warm and plesant now 1500 Rebel prissoners taken by General Banks 200 and 50 wounded Soldiers in the hospittle in N orlens.

MONDAY 20

is very warm Roomer in
Camp about our joining
the Regt again talk of goin
to join General Banks
Destruction of 6 or 8 Rebel gun
Boats

April 20, 1863 – is very warm   Roomers in Camp about our joining the Regt again talk of goin to join General Banks Destruction of 6 or 8 Rebel gun Boats.

TUESDAY 21

is very warm to Day our
Company C and B joind
the Regt to Day Co K took
our place I shal leave my
privet home and join my Co
to the Regt to Day I think

April 21, 1863 – is very warm to Day   our Company C and B joined the Regt to Day Co K took our place I shal leave my privet home and join my Co to the Regt to Day I think.

April 22, 1863 – it is very warm to Day I Did not go to the Regt yesterday I hav bin playing the fiddell I shal go to Camp to Day for the first time Since March the 30th to Stay all night.

McGregor recalls: "The One Hundred and Twenty-eighth New York returns from its excursion across the lakes. It was a raid on the enemy, which was very successful, capturing and destroying large amounts of Confederate property. General Banks is freeing all the southern and western parts of the state of enemies, preparatory to a great movement, in conjunction with General Grant, for opening the Mississipi.

McGregor's remarks speak of preparations for the assault on Port Hudson that will come in just a matter of a few weeks. Boredom will soon come to a screeching halt and for those soldiers that survive, life will never be the same again.

April 23,1863 – is not very plesant it Rained very hard last night I go wet and Caught a very bad Could and hav got a Sore throat.

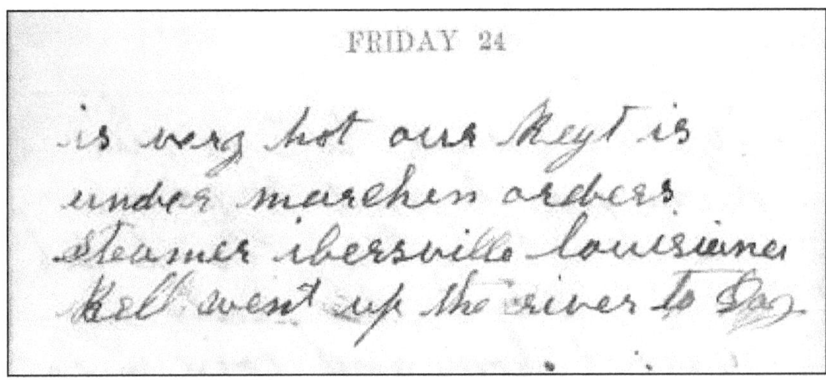

FRIDAY 24

is very hot our Regt is
under marchen orders
Steamer ibersville louisiana
Bell went up the river to Day

April 24, 1863 – is very hot our Regt is under marchen orders Steamer ibersville louisianer Bell went up the river to Day.

Orders were received to prepare to move on a moment's notice with two days' rations, the general feeling of the troops was that this meant that they would soon see action in the field. Excitement was beginning to grow in the ranks.

April SATURDAY 25 1863

is very hot the gun boat
poartsmouth has gon Down
the river She has bin anchored
in the Chanel of the river et the
parapet for 12 months She
Caries 22 = 42 pound guns

April 25, 1863 – is very hot the gun boat poartsmouth has gon Down the river She has bin anchored in the Chanel of the river et the parapet for 12 months She Caries 22 = 42 pound guns.

According to her records, the U.S.S. Portsmouth carried eighteen medium 32 pounder guns and two Paixhans 64 pounder shell guns.

SUNDAY 26

is warm hav writen to martha
to Day hav bin puting in a
Drum head for my self in
Carllton Smith Isaac helped me
we had som whiskey punch and
lemonade which was very good

April 26, 1863 - is warm hav written to Martha to Day hav bin putting in a new drum head in Carllton (?) Smith Isaac helped me we had some whiskey punch and lemonade which was very good.

MONDAY 27

is warm and plesant hav bin
to Camp to Day Charles
Cram went to the hospittle
George Bailey is in the
hospittle

April 27, 1863 – is warm and plesant hav bin to Camp to Day Charles Cram went to the hospittle George Bailey is in the hospittle.

Charles Cram (See Diary notes on June 16, 1863). George W. Bailey was from Lyman and enlisted as a private at age 27 and mustered into Company "C," 15th New Hampshire Volunteers on October 8, 1862. He was mustered out on August 31, 1863.

APRIL TUESDAY 28 1863

is hot to Day hav bin to Camp to Day General Banks arived to the Citty to Day with 200 Regulars no news of eny importence

April 28, 1863 – is hot to Day hav bin to Camp to Day General Banks arived to the Citty to Day with 200 Regulars no news of eny importence.

WEDNESDAY 29

in Carrlton to Day is warm and plesant hav bin loafing round the Street all Day Charles Cram is in the hospitle Sick and L. L. Terill

April 29, 1863 – in Carrlton to Day is warm and pleasant here been loafing round the Street all Day Charles Cram in the hospittle and L. L. Terill.

Levi L. Tyrrell was from Bethlehem and enlisted as a private at age 33 and mustered into Company "C," 15th New Hampshire Volunteers on October 8, 1862. He was mustered out on August 13, 1863.

THURSDAY 30

is a little Cooler to Day hav
bin up to Camp et the
parapet 2 germans Came to
Se me this Evning this
month has not Seamed So
long as March Did to me

April 30, 1863 – is a little Cooler to Day hav bin up to Camp et the parapet 2 germans Came to Se me this Evning this month has not Seamed So long as March did to me.

So ends the month of April and with the activities that took place during the month, Richard evidently did not suffer the boredom and loneliness that he felt earlier. Soon he and his comrades will be far from bored.

Chapter Five
May, 1863

Richard's unit was enlisted for a period of nine months and Richard was mustered into Company "C" on October 10, 1862. Six months have past since his enlistment and three months have been spent at camps and other locations in the New Orleans area. So far, the routine has been somewhat boring, oh sure – there were some periods of activity, but to date no military action with the enemy. What are we doing here? When are we going home?

BEFORE SEEING ACTIVE SERVICE.

In his book _Fate is the Hunter_, Ernest Gann defined flying as "...hours of boredom interspersed with moments of sheer terror..." Richard and his comrades were soon to learn that this definition applied to war as well. But in the meantime.........

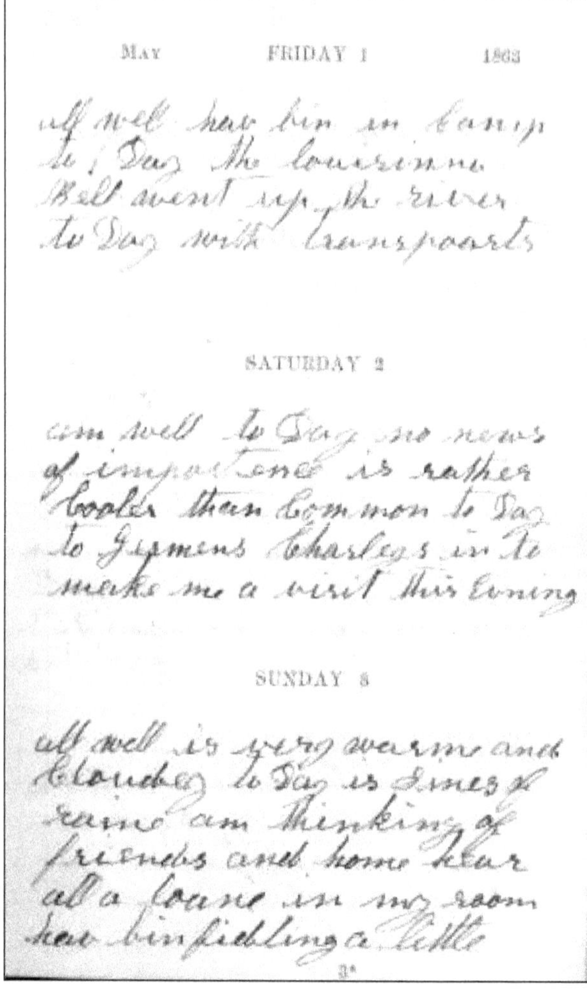
MAY FRIDAY 1 1863

all well hav bin in Camp to Day the louisianna Bell went up the river to Day with transpoarts

SATURDAY 2

am well to Day no news of importence is rather Cooler than Common to Day to Jermens Charleys in to make me a visit this Evning

SUNDAY 3

all well is very warm and Cloudey to Day is Sines of raine am thinking of friends and home hear all a loane in my room hav bin fidling a little

May 1, 1863 – all well hav ben in Camp to Day the louisianna Bell went up the river to Day with transpoarts

May 2, 1863 – am well to Day no news of importence is rather Cooler than Common to Day to Jermens Charleys in to make me a visit this Evning.

May 3, 1863 – all well is very warm and Cloudey to Day is Sines of raine am thinking of friends and home hear all a loane in my room has been fidling a little.

The first of May brings the same routine and Richard reports briefly on the weather and no real news to make note of. On the 3rd he does speak of loneliness and bides his time doing a little fiddling in his room.

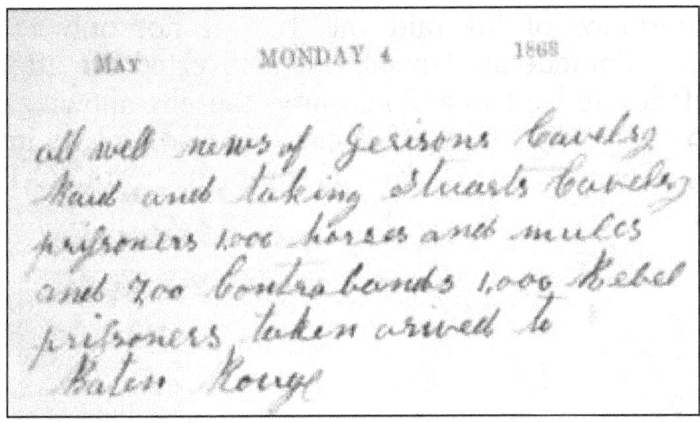
MAY MONDAY 4 1863

all well news of Gerisons Cavelry Raid and taking Stuarts Cavelry prisoners 1000 horses and mules and 700 Contrabands 1,000 Rebel prisoners taken arived to Baten Rouge

May 4, 1863 – all well news of Gerisons Cavelry Raid and taking Stuarts Cavelry prissoners 1,000 horses and mules and 700 Contrabands 1,000 Rebel prissoners taken arived to Baten Rouge.

McGregor comments: "Receive the news of the great Grierson cavalry raid, down from the North, through Mississippi to our lines. Greatest cavalry feat ever performed; great rejoicing."

Benjamin Henry Grierson enlisted on August 28, 1861 as a Major and on January 9, 1862 he was commissioned into Field and Staff in the Illinois 6th Cavalry. In the spring of 1863, he led his famous raid as part of General Grant's Vicksburg Campaign. Grierson left La Grange, Tennessee on the 17th of April with about 1,700 men and marched over 800 miles through enemy territory during the following seventeen days. During that time he and his men disabled railroads, captured prisoners, horses and equipment, destroyed property and finally ended up in Baton Rouge, Louisiana.

The importance of his raid was that it not only tended to demoralize Confederate troops, but it diverted the attention of the Confederate leaders at Vicksburg, thereby allowing General Grant to attack with more efficiency. He also took an important role in the siege at Port Hudson as commander of the XIX Corps Cavalry.

The photograph above is of Grierson's Cavalry being reviewed after their arrival at Baton Rouge.

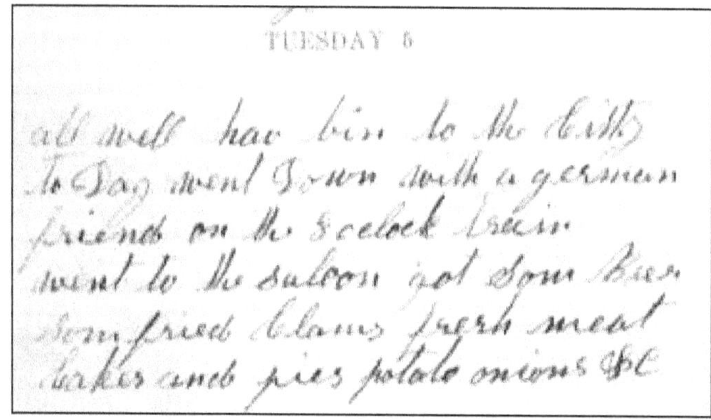

TUESDAY 5

all well hav bin to the Citty
to Day went Down with a german
friend on the 8 oclock train
went to the saloon got Som Beer
Som fried Clams fresh meat
Cakes and pies potato onions &c

April 5, 1863 – all well hav bin to the Citty to Day went Down with a german friend on the 8 o clock train went to the Saloon got Som Beer Som fried Clams fresh meat Cakes and pies potato onions etc.

In the Accounts section of his diary he notes on April 5th that he received $1.00 in camp funds; on the following day he notes that he paid $1.00 for Whiskey and Drinks of Beer, etc.

WEDNESDAY 6

May 6, 1863 - all is well Cooler to Day no news Co C has Received letters from home I. Smith Received one from amos I Did not get eny myself.

McGregor comments: "Boys all in high spirits. Our camp is delightful. The company streets are all roofed with canes and also the long regimental front, with seats beneath; the grounds are scrupulously clean. There are many unique features, especially about the officers' tents; some have raised beds of flowers."

MAY THURSDAY 7 1863

May 7, 1863 – all well is Cool to Day no news in Camp hav not Dun eny Dutey yet hav not Staid in Camp yet.

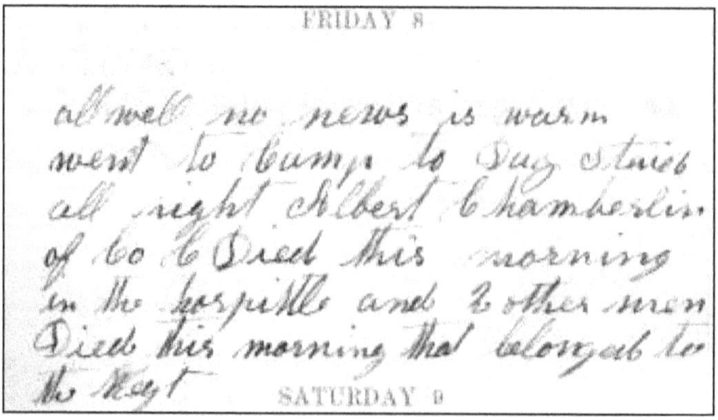
FRIDAY 8

all well no news is warm
went to Camp to Day Staid
all night Albert Chamberlin
of Co C Died this morning
in the hospittle and 2 other men
Died this morning that belonged to
the Regt

SATURDAY 9

May 8, 1863 – all well no news is warm went to Camp to Day Staid all night Albert Chamberlain of Company C died this morning in the hospittle and two other men died this morning that belonged to the Regt.

Albert Chamberlain was from Bath and enlisted as a private at age 18 and mustered into Company "C," 15th New Hampshire Volunteers on October 14, 1862. His records indicate that he died of disease on May 9, 1863 at Carrollton, Louisiana. He is buried in the Chalmette National Cemetery, Chalmette, Louisiana. – Gravesite 11-1032.

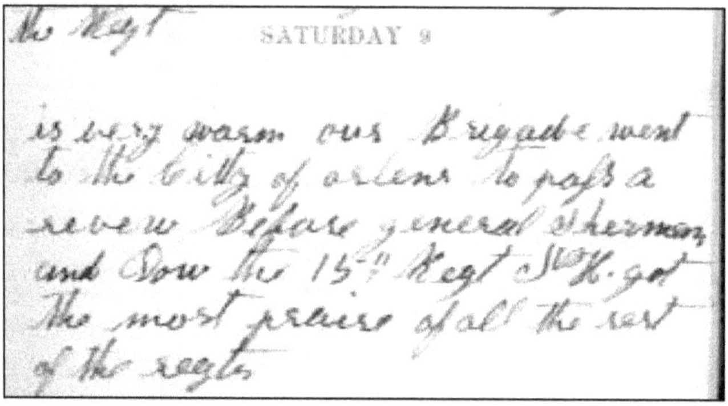
the Regt

SATURDAY 9

is very warm our Brigade went
to the Citty of orlens to pass a
revew Before general Sherman
and Dow the 15th Regt NH got
the most praise of all the rest
of the regts

May 9, 1863 – is very warm our Brigade went to the Citty of orlens to pass a revew Before general Sherman and Dow the 15th Regt NH got the most praise of all the rest of the regts.

McGregor describes the day and the event: "May 9, Saturday. Clear, bright and very warm. The grand feature of this day was the march of Sherman's army to New Orleans. One object of this may have been to show the Union strength and overawe the rebellious element of the great city, now soon to be left unprotected by the withdrawal of the troops to active service up the river. The secessionist had at times been somewhat demonstrative, and sedition and insurrection attempted. Our brigade formed at 7 o'clock near the old camp ground at Carrollton, two miles away on the shell road. Our regiment moved at daylight marching on the levee to Carrollton, Companies K and F joining us there. General Dow, surrounded by his staff, took command at that point; all in full, heavy marching order. It was the most magnificent pageant in which the Fifteenth Regiment had ever participated. Colors were flying and bands playing. The boys were permitted to sing along the route, and "Marching Along" and "Old John Brown" and many others were rendered with great effect.

The march was along the famous shell road. On entering the city, the strictest discipline is enforced, and the marching was perfect and the scene inspiring. The streets were thronged with gaily dressed people, mostly ladies. The march was continued through the principal streets; were received with cheers in many places. The great city was clean as a lady's parlor. Our bands played "Yankee Doodle" and all the national airs. General Sherman reviewed the army from his headquarters; all officers salute in passing, and the flags are dipped. The old general seemed greatly pleased, and praised the troops highly. It was a march of twenty miles."

MAY SUNDAY 10 1863

is warm and plesent Isaac Smith
has bin with me to Day we had
plenty of whiskey punch and a good
Diner the Brass Band is just
playing the Retreat from the Buriel
ground of Albert Chemberlain

May 10, 1863 – is warm and plesent Isaac Smith has bin with me to Day we had plenty of whiskey punch and a good Diner the Brass Band is just playing the Retreat from the Buriel ground of Albert Chemberlain.

May 11 – all well no news of eny importence is warm and Drye I. Smith Sends a letter to Amos to Day. James Garland Charles Cram is Down to Carrollton to Day.

May 12 – all well 2 ladies up from the Citty of N.orleans to Carlolt to Miss Grundies* on a visit had a good time no news of eny importence I went to Camp to Day.

James Garland was from Lyman, New Hampshire and was mustered into Company "C" 15th New Hampshire Infantry on October 8, 1862. Charles Cram was mustered into Company "C" 15th New Hampshire Infantry on October 8, 1862. He died of disease on July 24, 1863 at Port Hudson, Louisiana.

*Richard refers to Mrs. Grundies several times in his diary and also in his account records:

CASH ACCOUNT—MAY.

Date		Received.	Paid.
May 4th	to Mrs Grundy		2,00
5	for cars fare to N. Orleans		20
6th	Received from Government		5
	twenty 4 Dollars	24 00	10
15th	to Mrs Grundey		5,00
16th	for milk Whiskey		50
26th	for Whiskey 3 Pts		1,00
31st	for meals on Steam boat to N. Orleans		50
	for Whiskey in Carrollton and 3 meals of vidules		1,00
			4.35

In the accounting above, he shows a payment to her of $2.00 on the 4th and $5.00 on the 15th. On the 30th of March he shows a payment to a person unknown of $5.00 with the notation "..for Board and sickness..." It is possible that this woman owned the house where Richard was helped during his sickness – recall his notation on March 15th:

".....not So well to Day hav gon to a privat house was treated kndley by them the maid got me hot Sling and got me warm water to Soack my feet in on her own couch and git me a good Swet...."

He may also have boarded here for a while, recall his notes on April 21st:

".....I Shal leave my privet home and join my Co to the Regt. To Day I think....."

It could be that this "privet home" is that of Mrs. Grundies.

MAY WEDNESDAY 13 1863

all well no news to Day Recieved a letter from Martha from Littleton

THURSDAY 14

all well I went to Camp to stay for good one Gunboat went up the river To Day no more news to mention.

FRIDAY 15

all well no news hav bin in Camp all Day.

Pretty much the same routine during the past three days.

MAY SATURDAY 16 1863

all well hav bin on Duty to
Day for the furst time Since the
10th of last March had a fight
with the cook Dan Bedell took
a vote in the Company to put
him out of the Coockery

May 16, 1863 – all well hav bin on Duty to Day for the furst time Since the 10th of last March had a fight with the Cook Dan Bedell took a vote in the Company to put him out of the Coockery.

Daniel Bedell was from Bath, New Hampshire and enlisted on September 15, 1862 as a private. On October 8, 1862 he was mustered into Company C, 15th Regiment New Hampshire Infantry.

In many instances the soldiers cooked for themselves but in some companies cooks were "voted" into office, if they didn't perform as expected they were "recalled." The fare was limited by the situation, but hard tack, bacon (most times salt pork), beans and coffee were the main staples. In some areas wild game was available (recall Richard's alligator hunting expeditions) and occasionally fruits found in nature oranges, grapes, various species of berries made themselves available as well.

Officers generally ate much better than the men, this is reflected in the number of officers reporting for "sick bay" each month – food was among the prime culprits in sickness within the ranks.

SUNDAY 17

May 17, 1863 - is rainy today John Stuart and Dan B. Gage had a fight in our company to Day I am in good health in Camp now hav bin on Dutey all Day.

John Stuart was from Landaff and enlisted as a private at the age of 44 and mustered into Company "C," 15th New Hampshire Volunteers on October 8, 1862. His records indicate that he died of disease on July 31, 1863 at Memphis, Tennessee. Daniel B. Gage was from Enfield and enlisted as a private at age 41 and mustered into Company "C," 15th New Hampshire Volunteers on October 8, 1862. His records indicate that he died of disease on August 1, 1863 at Memphis, Tennessee.

MONDAY 18

May 18, 1863 – is warm the Steam Shipp George Cromwell arrived to Day with mail hav bin on brigade Drill to Day no news the band is playing, marching a long.

MAY TUESDAY 19 1863

May 19, 1862 – all well roomers in Camp of moveing hav bin on Dutey all Day 5 of our Company died we haveB buried 2 to Day Harry Chamberlain and Alson Littleton [Alson Little].

Harry Chamberlin was from Bath and enlisted as a private at age 24 and mustered into Company C," 15th New Hampshire Volunteers on October 8, 1862. His records indicate that he died of disease on May 18, 1863 at Carrollton, Louisiana. Alson S. Little was from Landaff and enlisted as a private at age 18 and was mustered into Company "C," 15th New Hampshire Volunteers on October 8, 1862. He was mustered out on August 13, 1863, evidently he wasn't one of the two buried on the nineteenth.

Ed. Note: The 1903 Guy S. Rix manuscript in the Lisbon Public Library, suggests that Alson Little is buried in Lisbon, NH – to date, attempts to locate his gravesite have been unsuccessful.

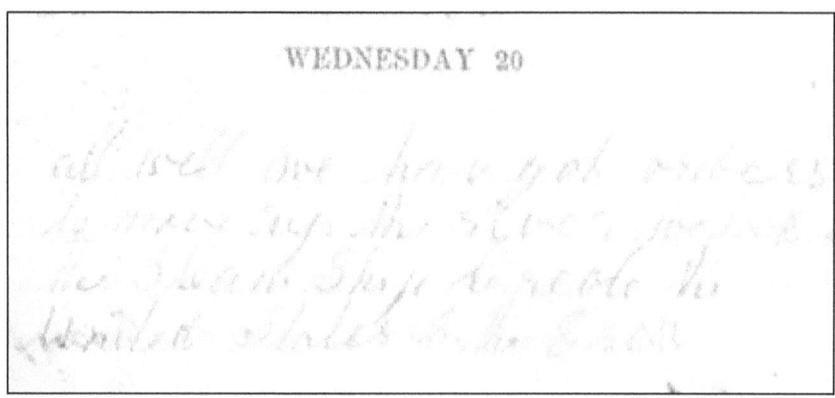
WEDNESDAY 20

May 20, 1863 – all well we hav got orders to move up the river we took the Steamship Creole the United States & the Esek [Essex]

Orders to move finally arrived and McGregor writes:

"May 20 was a very beautiful day, with a delightful breeze. General Sherman's division embarks at Carrollton for the siege of Port Hudson. When the order to move was received, eight companies, A, B, C, D, E, G, H, and I, were in the camp at the "Parapet," F and K were detached and on provost duty at Gretna across the river opposite New Orleans. At 5 o'clock in the afternoon Companies A, C, D, E, H and I broke camp, and with the band and colors marched to Carrollton under command of the colonel, his staff being present with him; B and G, under Osgood, followed an hour later. On arriving at the landing Companies A, B, D, E, F, G, H, and I marched aboard the ocean steamer "Crescent," upon which was already the Twenty-sixth Connecticut. Company "C" boarded the "United States," which was an ocean steamer also....."

After much preparation the steamers proceeded up the river toward Springfield Landing which was located on the east side of the river between Baton Rouge and Port Hudson.

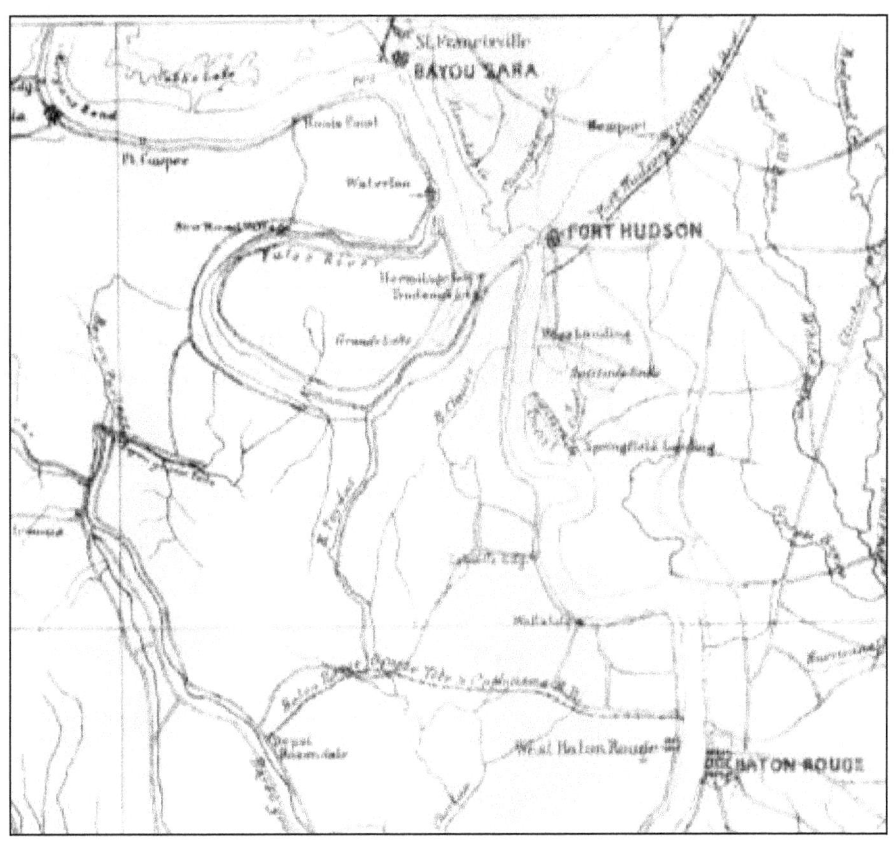

**Military Map of Part of Louisisana
Compiled at the
U. S. Coast Survey Office
A. D. Bache, Supt.
1863
(Author's collection)**

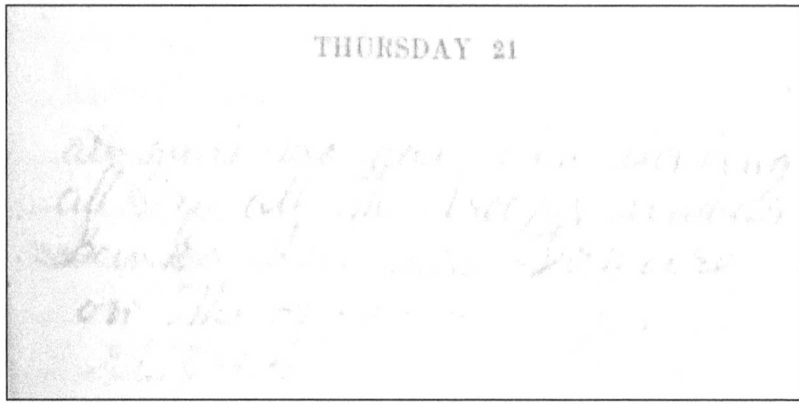

THURSDAY 21

May 21, 1863 – all well we have bin Sailing all Day all the troops under Banks Sherman Dow are on the move up the river.

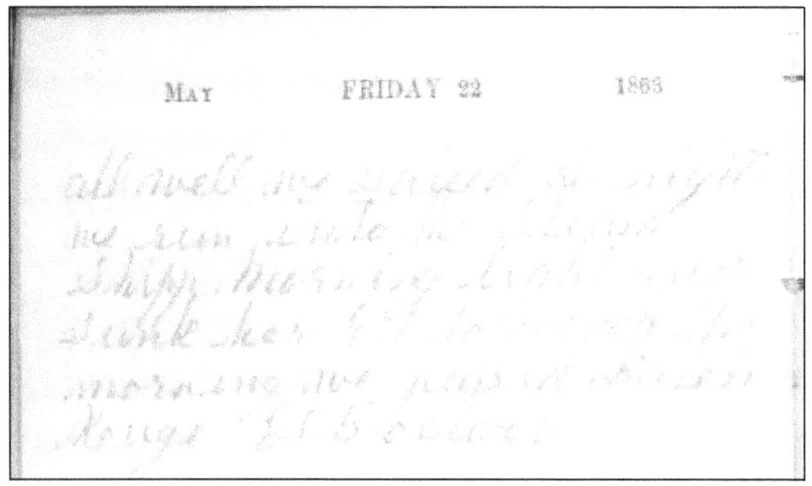

MAY FRIDAY 22 1863

May 22, 1863 – all well we sailed all night we run into the Steam Shipp Morning light and Sunk   Et to o clock this morning we passed Baon Rouge Et 5 o clock.....

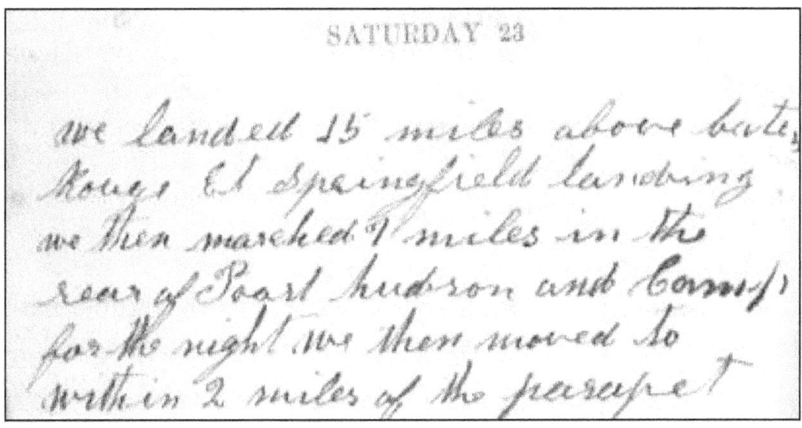

SATURDAY 23

we landed 15 miles above bate, Rouge et Springfield landing we then marched 7 miles in the rear of Poart hudson and Camp for the night we then moved to within 2 miles of the parapet

May 23, 1862 - .....we landed 15 miles above baten Rouge et Springfield landing we then marched 7 miles in the rear of Poart hudson and Camp for the night we then moved within 2 miles of the parapet.

Springfield Landing

Springfield Landing was located about five miles below the Confederate batteries at Port Hudson, in the artist's rendition pictured above you can faintly see the Union gunboats firing on the Confederate defenses.

There was evidence of warfare at the landing with many burnt-out buildings and other signs of military activity. Richard's regiment were among the first to come ashore with not much more than blankets, two-days rations of hard tack and 100 rounds of ammunition. To make matters a bit worse, there were constant showers along with plenty of heat. Now the reality of war is becoming evident.

From the landing the soldiers could easily hear the guns firing up ahead of them and it was obvious that the battle was underway, the heaviest of the guns came from Admiral Farragutt's war ships.

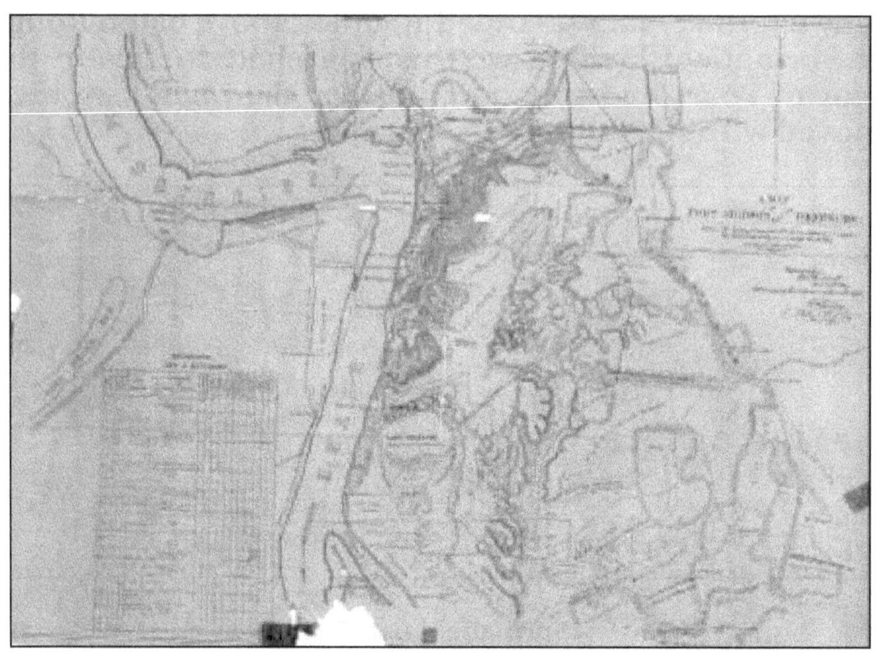

Leon J. Fremaux's Map of Port Hudson and its Defenses, 1862
(Gilmer Papers, Southern Historical Collection, University of North Carolina Wilson Library)

The Battle at Port Hudson was important because it essentially closed off the transportation of Confederate troops and supplies up and down the Mississippi River. The Union troops were under the command of Major General Nathaniel P. Banks and the Confederate troops under Major General Frank Gardner. General Gardner held onto his position until advised that General Grant and his forces had taken Vicksburg at which time he sent a series of messages to General Banks relative to articles of surrender and hostilities were ended at 6:00 o'clock A.M. on July 8, 1863.

The battle was actually conceived by General of the Army Winfield Scott who, although born in Virginia elected to remain loyal to the Union. He was a hero in the War of 1812 and commander of the U. S. Forces in the Mexican War and although he was almost 75 and in failing health at the time of the Civil War, his military mind was still as sharp as ever and President Lincoln made him General-in-Chief of the Union Forces.

General Scott, in 1861, weighed over 300 pounds and literally had to be hoisted on and off a horse in order to ride. None-the-less, he conceived of the Anaconda Plan which was adopted in 1862 and consisted of four parts.

THE PLAN:

1. Blockade the coasts of all of the seceding southern states in order to stop the flow of supplies and goods in and out.
2. Take control of the Mississippi River in order to cut the southern states off from the west.
3. Capture the Tennessee River, thereby dividing the south, and then marching through Georgia, thence proceeding to the coast.
4. Capture Richmond, Virginia, the capitol of the Confederacy.

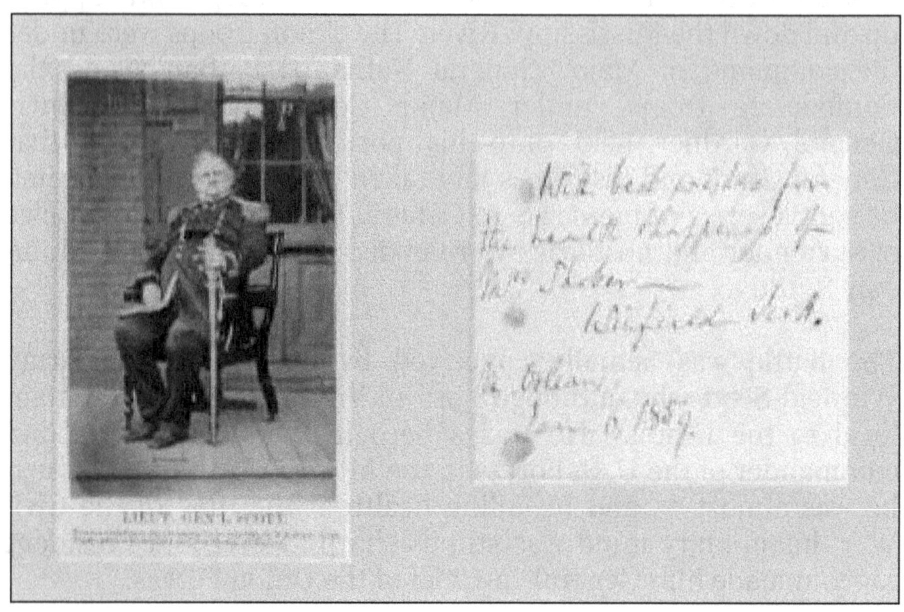

Lieutenant General Winfield Scott
(Author's collection)

General Scott's Anaconda Plan was not without critics, one was that it could not be implemented immediately because there were no warships of the size necessary to enforce a blockade were in existence. Further, most of his critics believed that a direct attack on the Confederate Capitol of Richmond would bring the war to an immediate end because if the capitol was taken, the Confederacy would soon collapse.

However, the war was not the brief encounter that his critics predicted and it was later shown that the plan was, in fact, a blueprint for victory for the Union even though that is still a matter of debate by military experts.

Several newspapers printed the cartoon illustrated below to show their distaste.

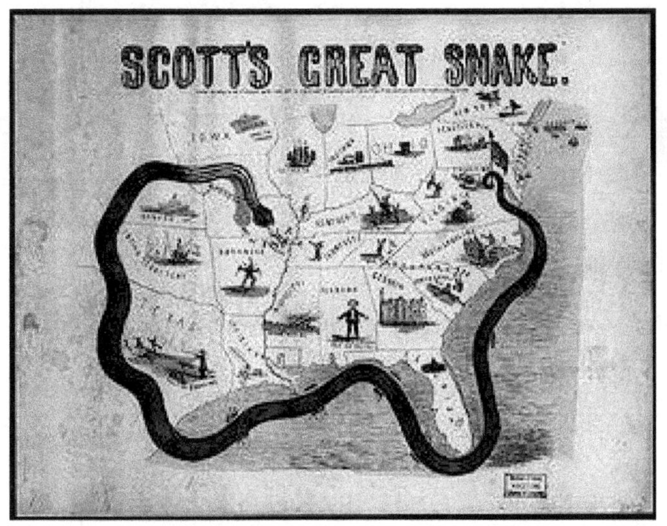

Although the plan was adopted with many reservations, it was put in place and the majority of the plan was the primary factor for the eventual Union victory. For the purposes of this writing the part of the plan that called for control of the Mississippi River is the focus.

The Battle of Vicksburg was, according to Confederate President Jefferson Davis, a "vital point" of the Confederacy. Although other areas of the war were more widely publicized, it was clear that if the Mississippi River was cut off it would allow Union forces free access to the South for troops and supplies.

So, with General Banks and Admiral Farragut attacking and eventually taking the Confederate defenses at Port Hudson in the southern portion of the river and General Grant attacking and finally taking Vicksburg in the north, the victories gave the Union full control of the river thereby striking a major blow to the Confederacy, which never recovered.

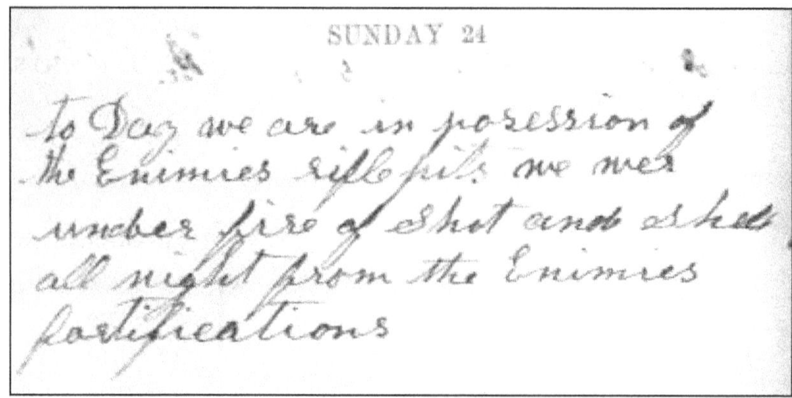

SUNDAY 24

to Day we are in possesion of
the Enimies rifle pits we wer
under fire of Shot and Shell
all night from the Enimies
fortifications

May 24, 1863 – to Day we are in possession of the Enimies rifle pits we wer under fire of Shot and Shell all night from the Enimies fortifications.

MAY MONDAY 25 1863

to Day we hav bin under fire
and all night thare has bin
heavey fireing and Canonading
all of the time on our Side
the 15 Regt NH Supports the Vt
1st Battery

May 25, 1863 – to Day we hav bin under fire and all night there has bin heavey fireing and Canonading all of the time on our Side the 15 Regt NH Supports the VT 1st Battery.

Major-General Nathaniel P. Banks was in command of the Nineteenth Army Corps and the Siege of Port Hudson. The First Division was under the command of Major General Christopher C. Auger and included three brigades, artillery and unattached units.

Richard's regiment was part of the First Brigade, Second Division – the Second Division was under the command of Brigadier General Thomas W. Sherman and the first brigade under Brigadier General Neal Dow. The first Vermont supplied the artillery.

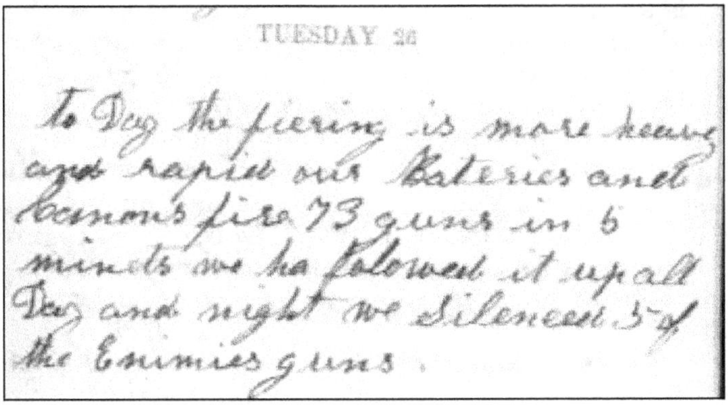
TUESDAY 26

to Day the fiering is more heavy and rapid our Bateries and Canons fire 73 guns in 6 minets we ha falowed it up all Day and night we Silenced 5 of the Enimies guns.

May 26, 1863 – to Day the fiering is more heavy and rapid our Bateries and Canons fire 73 guns in 5 minets we ha falowed it up all Day and night we Silenced 5 of the Enimies guns.

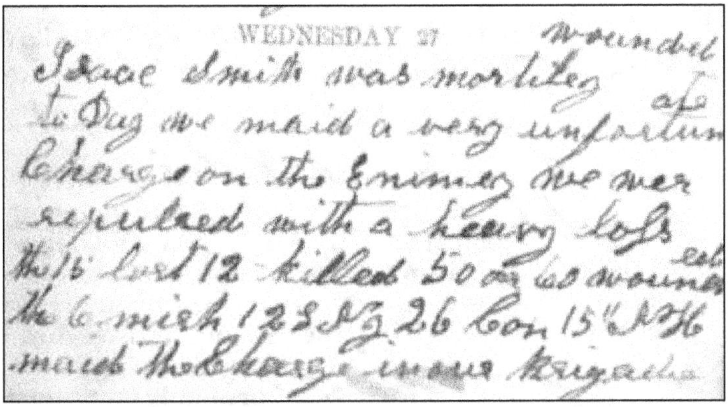
WEDNESDAY 27

Isaac Smith was mortiley wounded to Day we maid a very unfortunate Charge on the Enimey we wer repulsed with a heavy loss the 15 lost 12 killed 50 or 60 wounded the 6 mish 123 NY 26 Con 15 NH maid the Charge in our Brigade

May 27, 1863 - ....Isaac Smith was mortiley wounded to Day we maid a very unfortunate charge on the Enimey we wer repulsed with a heavy loss, the 15th lost 12 killed and 50 or 60 wounded the 6th mish., 123 NY, 26 Con 15th NH made the Charge in our Brigade.

Richard's brigade included the Twenty-sixth Connecticut, Sixth Michigan, Fifteenth New Hampshire, One Hundred and Twenty-eighth New York, One Hundred and Sixty-second New York.

McGregor recalls: "May 27 was a very beautiful day. The face of nature never shown more kindly down. It is high summer now, and there is an indescribable freshness and beauty in the tropical green wood where lie thousands all armed and panoplied in glittering steel and the habiliments of war.....From the earliest dawn, till night fell on the scene, the work of death went on. It was the commanding general's purpose to make a concerted movement on the enemy's works, but in this unity of action he signally failed, and it may be, thereby suffered disaster and defeat. The Third division, under General Paine, in which were eleven regiments and three batteries, advanced to the attack just at daybreak. On them the enemy were free to concentrate their fire, and they suffered immediate check but yet advanced to the very face of the parapet. The loss in this division is officially reported as 184 killed, 880 wounded, and 116 captured and missing; total, 1,180".

The Eighth New Hampshire Volunteers suffered the greatest losses of the day with a total of four officers and twenty-six men killed, seven officers and 191 men wounded, two officers and twenty-eight men captured or missing; total loss was 258.

Of particular note on this day is the story of the heroism of Corporal Enos K. Hall, Company "C" – 15th New Hampshire Volunteers:

CORP. ENOS K. HALL – CO. C.

McGregor writes: "Just after passing the little ravine and advancing upon the battle-field, McGregor, hearing shouts behind of 'Put up that flag,' tuned and saw Sergeant Merrick, having just regained his feet from the ravine, and having the flag gathered up around the staff and trailing it, which was probably the position in which he had to carry it through the brambles and general impediments which he had so far encountered; he was now in the act of unfurling it in that terrible storm, and it was instantly riddled with shot and torn to shreds.

The sergeant fell here; then Corporal McCluer, who just before the assault had been designated by Lieutenant Wyatt to represent Company B on the color guard, taking the flag from the fallen Merrick, fell off, with the rest, into the ravine, carrying the flag with him. He then took a position behind a near-by stump, and commenced firing upon the enemy; after two or three shots a comrade of the Twenty-sixth Connecticut called to hem, and asked if there was room for another there. He replied that there was, and then the Connecticut boy joined him, and they alternated firing over the stump; but after a very few rounds, while McCluer was down loading, the Connecticut boy, in the act of firing, received a shot directly in the centre of the forehead, and fell back dead across McCluer's legs, his blood and brains oozing out. McCluer laid him carefully aside, and went on with his work. Here Colonel Kingman approached, and asked where the color sergeant was. McCluer replied, 'Upon the field.' The colonel then asked if he was dead. McCluer said, 'No, but badly wounded.' He then called for volunteers to go with him – the colonel – to bring the sergeant in. McCluer went with the colonel, and taking each an arm, dragged the unfortunate sergeant from the field. The colonel then procured four with a stretcher to convey him to the surgeons.

Meanwhile Corp. Enos K. Hall of Company C, seized the flag, and bore it forward toward where Blair was rallying the men for another advance, when he, also, fell, very severely wounded. It is doubtful if a braver or more gallant deed than this was enacted that bloody day."

Enos K. Hall was from Landaff, New Hampshire and at age 31 enlisted as a Corporal on September 9, 1862, on October 8th he was mustered into Company C - 15th Regiment New Hampshire Infantry.

Pencil Sketch of a Portion of the Port Hudson Battlefield on May 27, 1863

MAY THURSDAY 28 1863

Isaac Smith Died Et 4 oclock this
morning on the road to Springfield
landing General Sherman was
wounded in the leg General Dow
was wounded. Liut Colonal blair
was wounded of the 14th Regt
and meny other officers

May 28, 1863 - Isaac Smith Died Et 4 o clock this morning on the road to Springfield landing, General Sherman was wounded in the leg, General Dow was wounded, Lt. Col. Blair was wounded of the 15th Regt. and many other officers.

Of note is that General Sherman was one of the wounded and treated at University Hospital in New Orleans. This General Sherman was Thomas West Sherman, who commanded the 2nd Division occupying the left flank of the Union lines at Port Hudson. The *Boston Evening Transcript*, June 6, 1863, notes: "On the enemy's right Gen. Sherman charged and carried the works by storm, but the enemy massed his troops and our men had to fall back. Gen. Sherman was seriously wounded in the leg."

In another section of the same paper, the following comment appears: "The GENERAL SHERMAN wounded at Port Hudson, is the Rhode Island and not the Ohio General of that name."

General Neal Dow was born in Portland, Maine and was commissioned as a Colonel in the 13th Maine Infantry on November 23, 1861 and on April 28, 1862 was promoted to Brigadier General; from February 26, 1863 he was attached to the Army and Department of the Gulf. He was wounded and taken prisoner during the siege of Port Hudson in 1863, and was exchanged for Confederate General W.H.F. Lee after an eight month imprisonment. After the war he ran for U.S. President in 1880 on the Prohibition ticket.

The letter below was signed by General Dow while at his headquarters at Camp Parapet in Carrollton, Louisiana; although post war letters signed by General Dow are somewhat common, those of war date are relatively rare.

Head Quarters US Forces Carrollton
Camp Parapet April 7th 1863

Captain

Private Berger wishes to rejoin his Regiment which is at or near Berwicks Bay. Be kind enough to give him an order for transportation to where ever his Regiment may be.

Very Respectfully
Neal Dow.
Brig Genl Comdg

Author's manuscript collection

LIEUTENANT-COLONEL BLAIR. (See page [illegible].)

Lieutenant Colonel Henry W. Blair was from Plymouth, New Hampshire and enlisted as a Major and was commissioned into Field & Staff New Hampshire 15th Volunteers. He was promoted to Lieutenant Colonel on April 8, 1863 and was severely wounded at Port Hudson on May 27, 1863 and again on June 14, 1863. He was mustered out on August 13, 1863.

Author's autograph collection

May 29, 1863 – to Day I hav written home and went Down to Carrollton on the Steam Ship and from there to neworlens after Some hospittle tents for the 15th Regt it is 1,45 (??) miles from Springfield to N orlens.

May 30, 1863 – to Day I went to Camp parapet after the tents and Returned to Carrollton Steam Boat landing Staid to Carrollton all night to my ould place.

"...my ould place..." Possibly Mrs. Grundies.

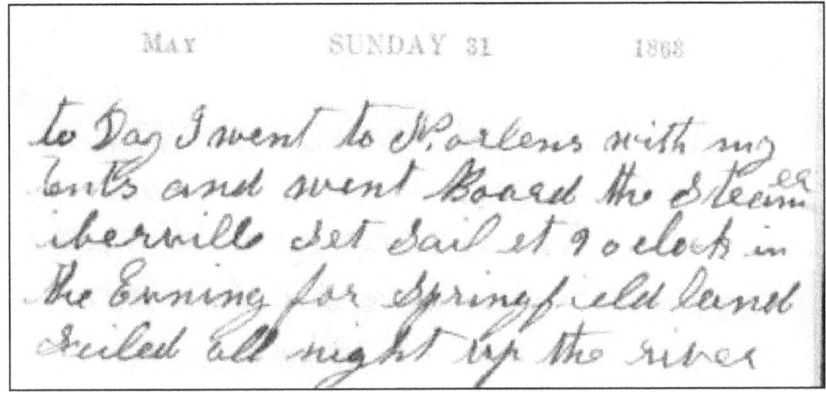

MAY SUNDAY 31 1863

to Day I went to N.orlens with my
tents and went Board the Steamer
iberville Set Sail et 9 o clock in
the Evning for Springfield land
Sailed all night up the river

May 31, 1863 – to Day I went to N.orlens with my tents and went Board the Steamer iberville Set Sail et 9 o clock in the Evning for Springfield land Sailed all night up the river.

Steamship "Iberville" – left

Relative to his boat trip, Richard notes in the Cash Account section of his diary for the 31st of May:

CASH ACCOUNT—MAY.

Date		Received.	Paid.
May 4th	to Mrs Grundy		2,00
5	for cars fare to N.orlens		20
6th	Received from Government		5
	twenty 4 Dollars	24 00	10
15th	to Mrs Grundey		5,00
16th	for milk Whiskey		50
26th	for Whiskey 3 Pts		1,00
31st	for meals on Steam boat to N.orlens		50
	for Whiskey in Carrollton and 3 meals of vidules		1,00
			10.35

For meals on Steam boat to N.orlens for Whiskey in Carrollton and 3 meals of vidules - $1.50

Chapter Six
June, 1863

JUNE MONDAY 1 1863

June 1, 1863 – to Day we landed et Baten Rouge et 12 o clock we then Set Sail and arived et Springfield landing et 4 o clock I then took the Bagage train for the Battle ground arived et 4 o c in the morning.

TUESDAY 2

June 2, 1863 – to Day I Deliverd the tents to the Generals head quarters and joined by Regt on the Battle ground our folks are fighting now in front of the enimey.

JUNE WEDNESDAY 3 1863

June 3, 1863 – to Day we are building fortifications for heavey Siege guns and morters we hav bin reinforcest with a good troops and Cannons we hav 150 Cannons and 80 Siege guns.

THURSDAY 4

June 4, 1863 – to Day our workes are progressing our fortifications are most all Completed although we hafto work under the fire of the enimey Sharp Shooters and Shells.

FRIDAY 5

June 5, 1863 – to Day the fireing Between the Sharp Shooters is very brisk I hav been out on an Excursion of Sharp Shooting for 24 hours 2 boys of our Regt was Badley wounded to Day 1 killed.

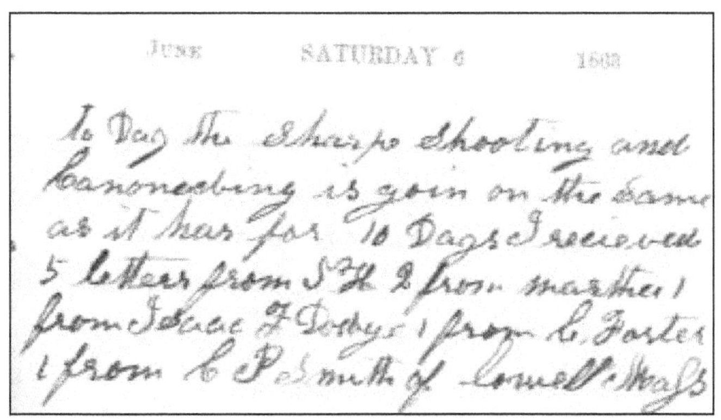

JUNE SATURDAY 6 1863

June 6, 1863 – to Day the Sharpe Shooting and Canonading is goin on the Same as it has for 10 Days I recieved 5 letters from NH 2 from Martha 1 from Isaac F. Dodge 1 from C Foster 1 from C P Smith of Lowell Mass.

Martha was discussed earlier; Isaac is Richard's brother Isaac F. Dodge. Isaac was also from Lyman and at age 30 he enlisted as a private, on September 19, 1862. He was mustered into Company "D" of the 13th Regiment New Hampshire Infantry, and was mustered out on June 21, 1865. Note that the postmark on the envelope is April 30, 1863 and the date received and notation in Richard's diary was June 6, 1863.

About the time that Isaac wrote his letter to Richard, his unit was attached to the 3rd Brigade, 2nd Division, 7th Corps, Army of the Department of Virginia. They were engaged in the Siege of Suffolk, April 12 through May 4th.

C. Foster was probably Charles Foster of Lowell, Massachusetts – an educated guess would be that he was a cousin or perhaps an uncle. Recall earlier notations about locating his Uncle Joseph Foster's grave at Carrollton. C. P. Smith's identity is unknown.

SUNDAY 7

to Day we are under fire from
the enimey our Canons are in
motion all the time Day and
night the fireing was very
heavey last night our men
are on Dutey all the time

June 7, 1863 – to Day we are under fire from the enimey our Canons are in motion all the time Day and night the fireing was very heavey last night our men are on Dutey all the time.

MONDAY 8

to Day is the Same we hav
bin building fortifications
and rifle pits in front of
the enimies works

June 8, 1863 – to Day is the Same we hav bin building fortifications and rifle pits in front of the enemies works.

JUNE TUESDAY 9 1863

to Day we are Shelling the
Rebels we Shal Soon be ready
to make another Charge
on thier workes I hope we Shal
hav better luck next time

June 9, 1863 – to Day we are Shelling the Rebels we Shal Soon be ready to make another Charge on thier workes I hope we Shal have better luck next time.

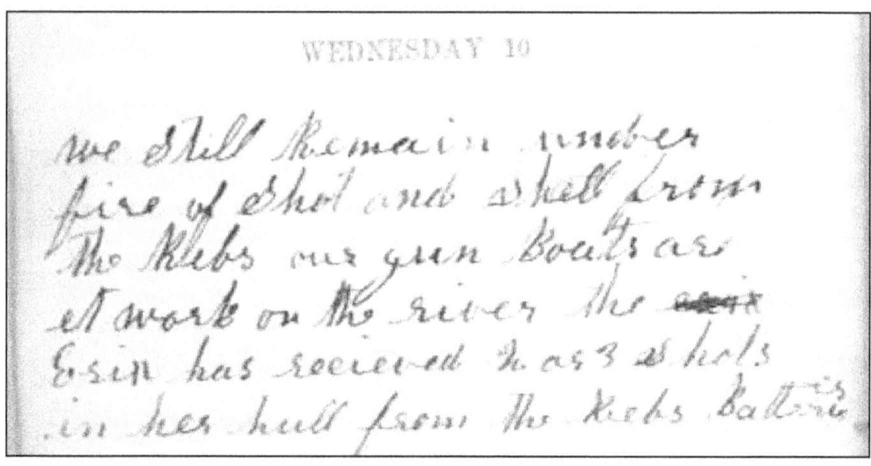

WEDNESDAY 10

we Still Remain under
fire of Shot and Shell from
the Rebs our gun Boats are
et work on the river the [illegible]
Erin has recieved 2 or 3 Shots
in her hull from the Rebs Batteries

June 10, 1863 – we Still Remain under fire of Shot and Shell from the Rebs our gun Boats are et work on the river the Erin has recieved 2 or 3 Shots in her hull from the Rebs Batteries.

A portion of a letter from Lieutenant Perkins, Company H, reads as follows:

Camp before Port Hudson, June 10, 1863

Dear Wife:

I wrote you about ten days since, but had some doubts about your ever getting the letter, or this either, as the report here is that letters are not allowed to go North at present. There is nothing of importance transpired since I wrote. We have got the rebels shut up as tight as a rat in a trap, and are bound to bag them before we leave them. I don't see any possible chance for them to escapee. We are building batteries and digging rifle pits all around them, and in a day or two I expect there will be one of the most terrific bombardments that has ever been known. Our rifle pits are within rifle shot of their parapet; we have been at work on them night and day. Their sharpshooters are firing at us all the time, and the balls are whizzing over our heads, but they don't hit many. They also give us a shower of shells and grape, but we give them back ten fold. There is scarcely five minutes, day or night, but that we hear the roar of artillery, or the bursting of shells. A good many deserters come in from the fort, and according to their reports the rebels have about six thousand men, with pretty good supply of provisions, and plenty of ammunition for small arms, but are short of large. They say also that a great many would leave if they could get away, and that many of the officers are in favor of surrendering. The day that we buried our dead a good many of them came and talked with us and appeared very friendly; shook hands with us when they left, telling us that if they took any of us prisoners they should use us well, and requested us to do the same by them. The night after the battle some of the wounded were left on the field, and the rebel surgeons went out and dressed their wounds, and told our pickets to bring water and they would not be fired on. One of our rifle pits runs across the battle-field. I expect our regiment will go into one of them tomorrow.

It is interesting to read about the compassion of the surgeons and the relative friendship of the troops during a cease-fire, after which it was business as usual.

THURSDAY 11

June 11, 1863 – to Day is rainey it thunders very heavey heavens artillery and Bankes is et work to geather 1 of our men killed to Day 2 wounded.

JUNE FRIDAY 12 1863

June 12, 1863 – to Day our folks are getting ready to make a Charge on the enimey our Soldiers Slept on thier alms all night til 1 o clock then we wer ordered to the left 2 or 3 miles the 15th NH and...........

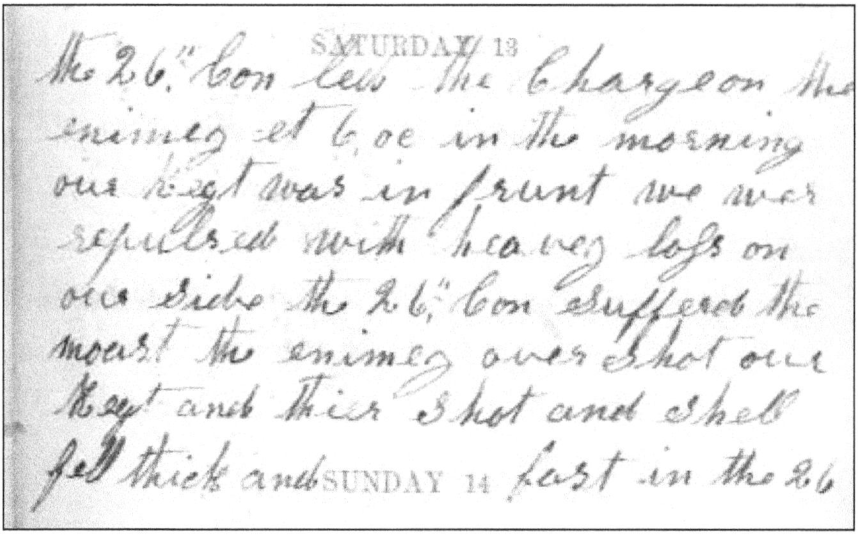

SATURDAY 13

the 26th Con led the Charge on the
enimey et 6 o c in the morning
our Regt was in frunt we wer
repulsed with heavey loss on
our Side the 26th Con Suffered the
moast the enimey over Shot our
Regt and thier Shot and Shell
fell thick and SUNDAY 14 fast in the 26

June 13, 1863 – the 26th Con led the Charge on the enimey et 6 o c in the morning our Regt was in frunt we wer repulsed with heavey loss on our Side the 26th Con Suffered the moast the enimey over shot our Regt and thier Shot and Shell fell thick and fast in the 26............

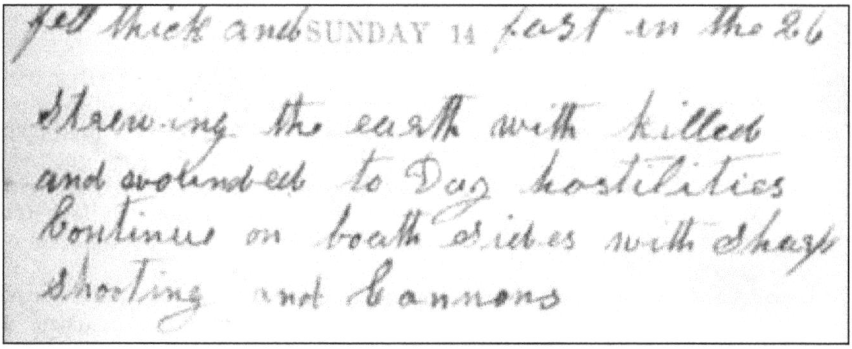

fell thick and SUNDAY 14 fast in the 26

Strewing the earth with killed
and wounded to Day hostilities
Continue on boath Sides with Sharp
Shooting and Cannons

June 14, 1863 - ....Strewing the earth with killed and wounded to Day hostilities Continue on boath Sides with Sharp Shooting and Cannons.

June 15, 1863 – to Day the Same as yesterday the workers of Death and Destruction is goin on more or less of our men killed every Day our Regt Still Remaines on the left in front of the enemies works.

The scene was one of constant shelling that continued throughout the day and night, a description of the events by Quartermaster Fred E. Smith, Eighth Regiment – Vermont Volunteers pretty much tells the story:

"Our officers and men lie quietly down, day and night, week after week, with hundreds of rifle-balls whistling within a few feet, often a few inches of their heads. And when, from necessity, they must leave their posts, they have to crawl behind logs, and through ditches and ravines to get to the woods in the rear. Perhaps on their way they must cross a knoll or a ridge of land, when – whist! whist! Whiz-z-z! go a half dozen bullets from sharpshooters, who are constantly watching every such exposed place.

The men of this command have been confined for more than a month to the ditches in which they live, sleep, eat and fight. In front are embankments of their own building, on the top of which are sand-bags and logs, forming loopholes through which they watch the enemy, and shoot at the sight of anything that moves. These are, in many places within twenty rods [100+ yards] of the earthworks behind which lie the enemy, keeping as close watch of us as we do of them. A continued roar of musketry is kept up on both sides while the bullets clip the leaves and branches overhead almost constantly. Along a large part of the line the men are obliged to approach the trenches crawling on their hands and knees.

Here, too, they sleep, if they sleep at all, in such an inclined position that morning finds them several feet lower down the bank than when they lay down. If the night be ever so rainy, all they can do is to lie or stand and take it. When the ground gets very slippery, so that they slide too much, they must drive some stakes to brace their feet against. Many of the men have dug holes in the bank large enough to admit their whole bodies, so that they literally live in caves of the earth. The cooking has to be done half or three-quarters of a mile in the rear, our of range of the guns, the food is carried in by cooks and negroes. You can easily imagine the men are of necessity very dirty and ragged, for their clothes soon get terribly filthy, or wear out. So much is their appearance altered that you would recognize but few of the men or officers of the old Eighth. Occasionally, a few get out, stretch their legs and get washed, and those who are fortunate enough to possess a change of shirt, put on a clean one. But as a rule the poor boys are unshaven, their hair is long and frequently uncombed for a week or more; and if close inspection were made, it might surprise their wives or mothers to find vermin living on their heads and bodies. Their food is, of course, very plain and very poor. The water they get is very bad even for this country, and the best they are able to procure would be thought unfit for cattle in Vermont. This is the actual state of things, only a deep shade too faintly pictured."

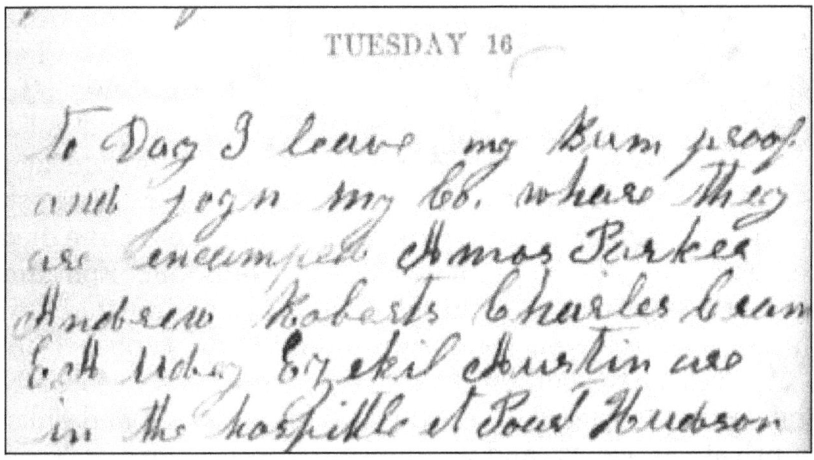

TUESDAY 16

To Day I leave my Bum proof
and jogn my Co. where they
are encamped Amos Parker
Andrew Roberts Charles Cram
E A Udey Ezekil Austin are
in the hospille at Port Hudson

June 16, 1863 - ....to day I leave my Bum proof and join my Co. where they are encamped, Amos Parker, Andrew Roberts, Charles Cram, E. A. Uudy, Ezekiel Austin are in the hospital at Port Hudson.

Amos V. Parker (below) was from Lyman and enlisted as a corporal on September 1, 1862, at age 37. He was mustered into Company "C," 15th New Hampshire Infantry on October 8, 1862. He died of disease on September 9, 1863 at Baton Rouge, Louisiana.

Andrew J. Roberts was from Enfield and enlisted as a private at age 42 and mustered into Company "C," 15th New Hampshire Infantry on October 8, 1862. His records indicate that he died of disease on August 13, 1863. Charles Cram was from Lyman and enlisted as a private at age 29, and was mustered into Company "C." 15th New Hampshire Infantry on October 8, 1862. His records indicate that he died of disease on July 24, 1863 at Port Hudson, Louisiana. Ephraim A. Eudy, age 25, was from Bethlehem and was mustered into Company "C," 15th New Hampshire Infantry on October 8, 1862, he was mustered out on August 13, 1863 at Concord, New Hampshire. Ezekiel E. F. Austin was from Enfield and enlisted as a private at age 37, and was mustered into Company "C," 15th New Hampshire Infantry on October 8, 1862. He was mustered out on August 13, 1863 at Concord, New Hampshire.

Amos Parker photograph – Author's Collection

“Bomb proofs” were most times nothing more than roofed shelters dug into the sides of hills; they did little or nothing to protect from direct hits bombs but did offer some protection from the fallout from the explosion. Some were a bit “fancier” than others and some were many times used as “hospitals” at Port Hudson.

This “bomb proof” is quite a bit fancier than the one above and has doors and apparently either a fireplace or some kind of stove – almost all the “comforts of home.”

WEDNESDAY 17

to Day is very hot no very hard fighting to Some Shelling and Sharp Shooting going on

June 17, 1863 – to Day is very hot no very hard fighting to Some Shelling and Sharp Shooting going on.

JUNE THURSDAY 18 1863

is rainey to Day the work goes rather slow to Day Some Rebs has Come out of the foart into our lines there is much talk of goin home in our Regt it is time we wer on the way now

June 18, 1863 – is rainey to Day the work goes rather slow to Day. Some Rebs has Come out of the foart into our lines there is much talk of goin hom in our Regt it is time we were on the way now.

It was reported that numerous confederate soldiers were breaking rank and surrendering to the Union forces.

FRIDAY 19

last night and to Day our
folkes has bin building
fortifications for large Siege
guns and making preperations
for a nother Charge on the
enimeys fortifications

June 19, 1863 – last night and to Day our folks has bin building fortifications for large Siege guns and making preperations for a nother Charge on the enimeys fortifications.

SATURDAY 20

to Day is very hot and the
time ways Slowley away now
I am to work in the Coockery
to Day hav built a little Cane
Brake house to Shed rain
and keep off the heavy Dew

June 20, 1863 – to Day is very hot and the time ways Slowly away now I am to work in the Coockery to Day hav built a little Cane Brake house to Shed rain and keep off the heavy Dew.

June 21, 1863 – to Day is the Same as yesterday hot and Dry our folkes are Still fortifying and Diging rifle pits 3 of the Vermont 14 Battery Boys were killed to Day by a Shell from the Rebs Batteries.

June 22, 23, 1863 – to Day is a little Cooler it rained last night I went all over our fortifications to Day on the left we were in talking Distence from the Rebs our folkes are planting very heavey Siege guns to Day one weighs 16, 337 lbs and one large perrot rifle 32 lbs gun 4 morters 10 inch Shell 4 large howitzers 9 inch and a number of other guns of Diferent sises for grape and Canister the works are all Compleated on the left next to the river for action.

JUNE WEDNESDAY 24 1863

to Day the Rebs hoisted thier flag
and gaves us 3 shots to let us no
that they wer Ready for us but we
soon loard her flag with our 32 lb
rifle gun one shot took her flag from
her mast which Settled the fuss to Day

June 24, 1863 – to Day the Rebs hoisted thier flag and gaves us 3 shots to let us no that they wer Ready for us but we soon loard her flag with our 32 lb rifle gun one Shot took her flag from her mast which Settled the fuss to Day.

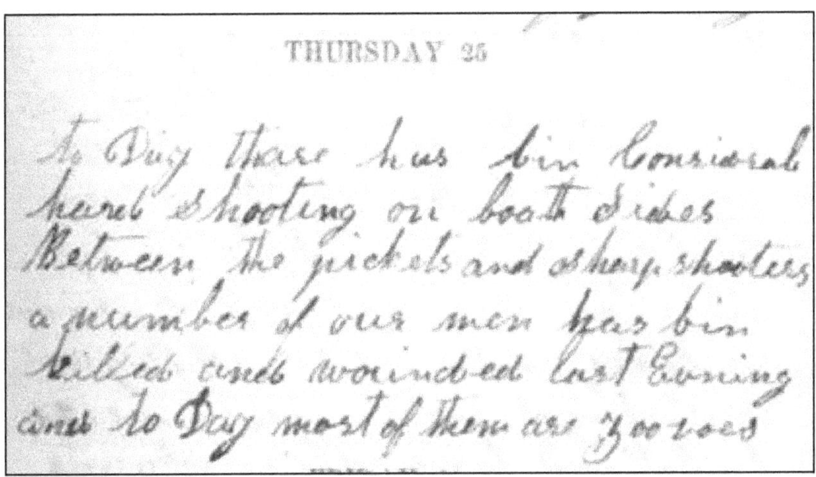

THURSDAY 25

to Day there has bin Considerabl
hard Shooting on booth Sides
Between the pickets and sharp shooters
a number of our men has bin
killed and wounded last Evning
and to Day most of them are Zoovoes

June 25, 1863 – to Day there has bin Considerable hard Shooting on both Sides Between the pickets and Sharp Shooters a number of our men has bin killed and wounded last Evning and to Day most of them are zoovoes.

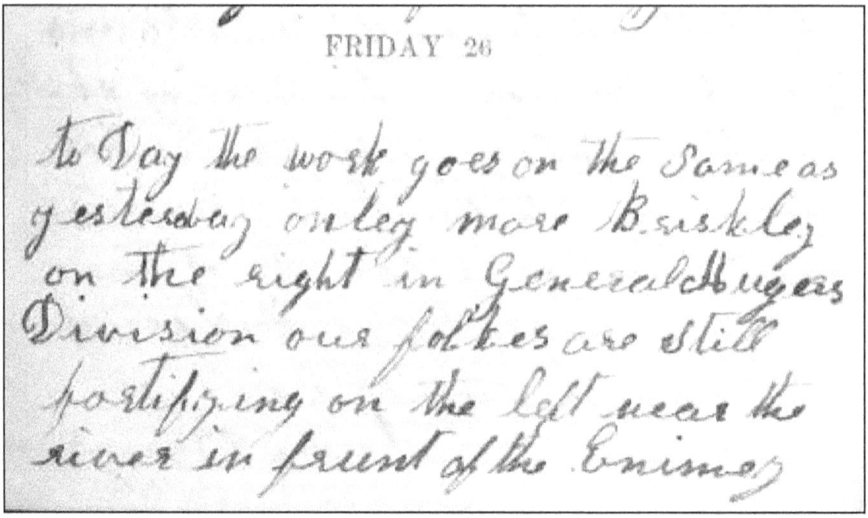
FRIDAY 26

to Day the work goes on the Same as yesterday onley more Briskley on the right in General Hughes Division our folkes are Still fortifying on the left near the river in frunt of the Enimey

June 26, 1863 – to Day the work goes on the Same as yesterday onley more Briskley on the right in General Hughes Division our folkes are Still fortifying on the left near the river in frunt of the Enimey.

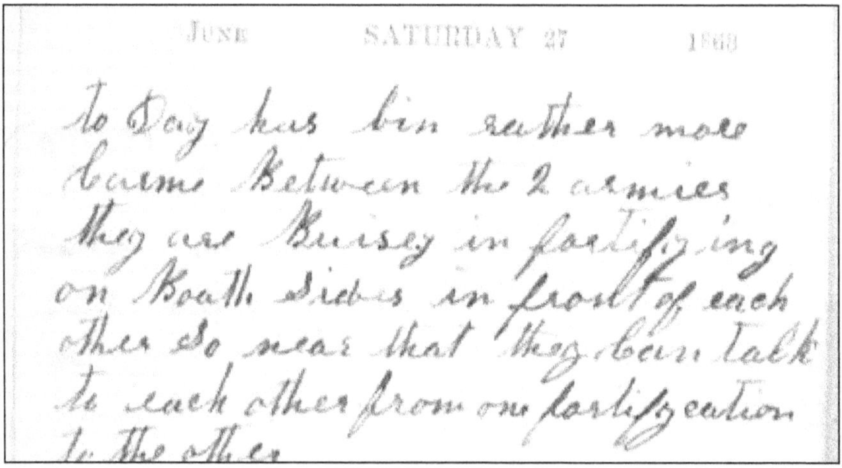
JUNE SATURDAY 27 1863

to Day has bin rather more Carme Between the 2 armies they are Buisey in fortifying on Boath Sides in front of each other So near that they Can talk to each other from one fortification to the other

June 27, 1863 – to Day has bin rather more Carme Between the 2 armies they are Buisey in fortifying on Boath Sides in front of each other So near that they Can talk to each other from one fortification to the other.

Interior View of the Confederate Fortifications at Port Hudson

SUNDAY 28

To Day the Bombarding has bin kept up with the Big Battery on the Left and the Gun Boats in the river from the Esix and the Richmond our Battery on the left has got 15 guns consisting of heavy Siege guns 120 lbs Ball and large rifle perrot guns and 96 lbs morters for throeing shell another Battery to the right of that of 6 guns 32 lbs Brass Cannons Still to the right on the Same line another large Battery of 12 guns all of which is in our Division numbering 33 guns in all

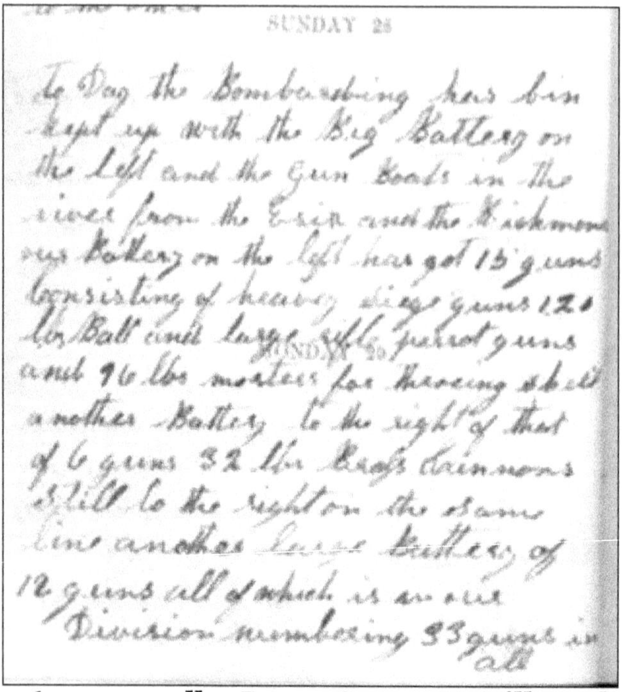

June 28, 29, 1863 – to Day the Bombarding has bin kept up with the Big Battery on the left and the Gun Boats in the river from the Esix and the Richmond our Battery on the left has got 15 guns consisting of heavy Siege guns 120 lb Ball and large rifle perrot guns and 96 lbs morters for throeing shell another Battery to the right of that of 6 guns 32 lbs Brass Cannons Still to the right on the Same line another large Battery of 12 guns all of which is in our Division numbering 33 guns in all.

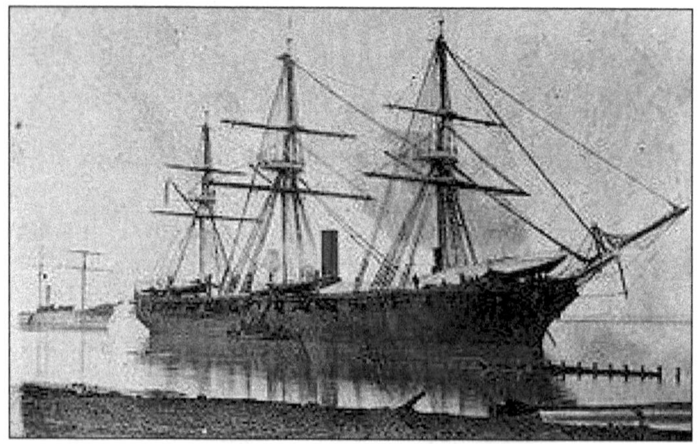

The USS Richmond was a wooden steam sloop that was commissioned in 1860 with a displacement of 2,604 tons and a length of 225 feet, top speed was 9 knots. The armament included: 1 80 pounder Dahlgren smooth bore, 20 9" Dahlgren smooth bore, and one 30 pounder Parrott rifle.

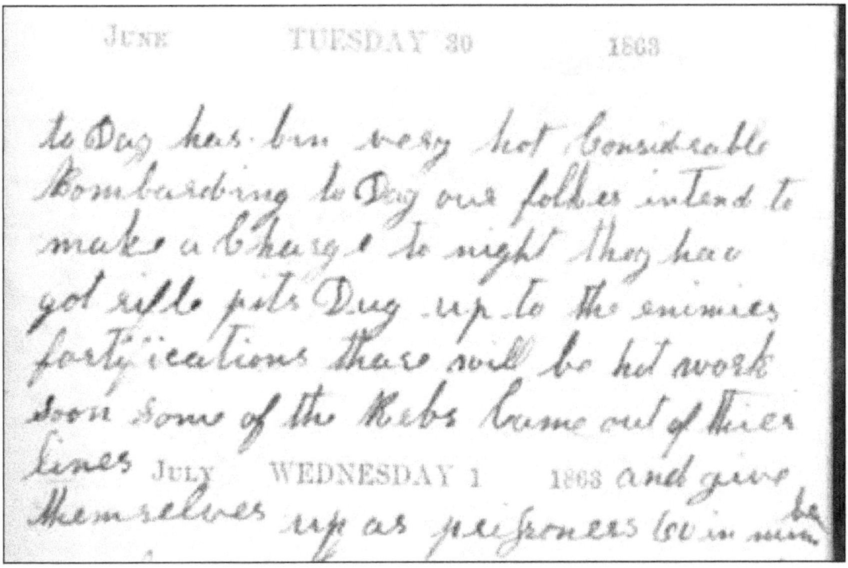

June 30, 1863 – to Day has bin very hot Considerable Bombarding to Day our folkes intend to make a Charge to night they hav got rifle pits Dug up to the enemies fortifications those will be hot work Soon Some of the Rebs Came out of thier lines and give themselves up as prissoners.

Chapter Seven
July, 1863

lines JULY WEDNESDAY 1 1863 and give
themselves up as prisoners 60 in num be
one of our Comp was wounded to
Day and 3 others in the Regt
William P Gillman was one from
our Comp a number of our Boys
gets Sun Struck every Day the
Bombarding Continues to Day
we hav had THURSDAY 2 Some truble
with the Gorillers in our rear
to Day but we Soon maid them
Scheedaddle it is very hot and
our men are failing fast our
Regt Reporarts onley 270 for
Dutey our Company onley 45 for
Dutey

July 1, 1863 – one of our Camp was wounded to Day and 3 others in the Regt William P. Gillman was one from our Camp a number of our Boys gets Sun Struck every Day The Bombarding Continues to Day.

William P. Gilman was from Tamworth and at age 41 was mustered into Company C, 15th New Hampshire Volunteers on November 5, 1862, he was mustered out on August 13, 1863.

July 2, 1863 – we hav had Some truble with the Gorillers in our rear to Day but we Soon maid them Scheedadle it is very hot and our men are failing fast our Regt Reporarts only 270 for Dutey our Company only 45 for Dutey.

JULY FRIDAY 3 1863

to Day the Battle goes about the Same
I had a variety for Diner to Day Some
fried liver and Beef Stake the first
for 44 Days that we hav taisted fresh
meat General Banks is reported
very Sick to Day our men are tunil
ing under the Rebs works

SATURDAY 4

to Blow them up this morning we
had Baked Beens and meat for
Breakfust our time is Said to Be
to Day our Beens wer Baked in a
hole in the ground no atatet has
Bin Maid to Day for the tuniling
was not ready for blowing them up

July 3, 1863 – to Day the Battle goes about the Same I had a variety for Diner to Day Some fried liver and Beef Stakes the first for 44 Days that we hav taisted fresh meat General Banks is reported very Sick to Day our men are tuniling under the Rebs works to Blow them up.

July 4, 1863 – this morning we had Baked Beens and meat for Breakfast our time is Said to Be to Day our Biens are wer Baked in a hole in the ground no ??? has Bin Maid to Day for the tuniling was not ready for blowing them up.

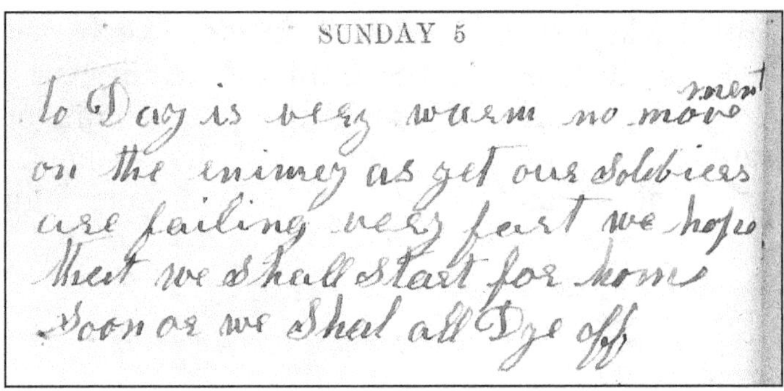

SUNDAY 5

to Day is very warm no movement
on the enimey as yet our Soldiers
are failing very fast we hope
that we Shall Start for home
Soon or we Shal all Dye off

July 5, 1863 – to Day is very warm no movement on the enimey as yet our Soldiers are failing very fast we hope that we Shall Start for home Soon or we Shal all Dye off.

JULY MONDAY 6 1863

to Day we hav good news
from Vicksburg General
Banks has Recieved orders
from General Grant that
Vicksburg has Did Surender
the 4th at 10 oclock Salutes were
fiard at TUESDAY 7 Poart
Hudson in all of our Divisions
the Rebs thought all hell was
let loose when the Saluting
begun they all Scheedaddled to
thier Strong holds and Did
not Come out till the Salutes
was over

July 6 & 7, 1863 – to Day we hav good news from Vicksburg General Banks Recieved orders from General Grant that Vicksburg Did Surender the 4th at 10 o clock Salutes were fiard at Port Hudson in all our Divisions the Rebs thought all hell was let loos when the Saluting begun they all Scheedaddled to thier Strong holds and Did not Come out till the Salutes was over.

The fall of Vicksburg to General Grant's forces essentially sounded the death knell for the Confederates at Port Hudson. On July 7th, Major-General Frank Gardner, commanding the Confederate forces, wrote a letter to Major-General Banks requesting "official" confirmation that Vicksburg indeed had fallen.

General Banks responded as follows:

"In reply to your communication, dated the seventh instant, by flag of truce received a few moments since, I have the honor to inform you that I received yesterday morning, July 7, at 10:45 o'clock, by the gunboat 'General Price,' an official dispatch from Major-General Ulysses S. Grant, U. S. Army, whereof the following is a true extract:

'....General: The garrison of Vicksburg surrendered this morning. Number of the prisoners as given by the officers is 27,000, field artillery 128 pieces, and a large number of siege guns- probably not less than 80.

U. S. Grant, Major-General'"

After several communications passed between Banks and Gardiner, Gardiner wrote back requesting a suspension of hostilities and a designated area where the terms of the surrender of the Confederate troops of Port Hudson could be drawn up.

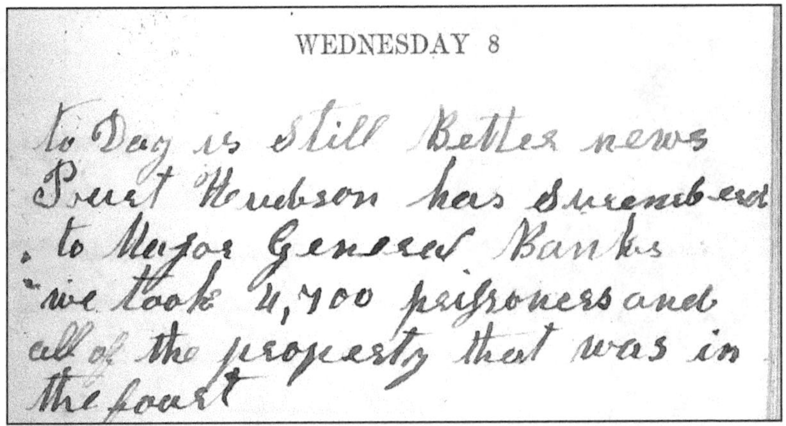
WEDNESDAY 8

to Day is Still Better news
Pourt Hudson has Surenderd
to Major General Banks
we took 4,700 prissoners and
all of the property that was in
the foart

July 8, 1863 – to Day is Still Better news Pourt Hudson has Surendered to Major General Banks we took 4,700 prissoners and all of the property that was in the foart.

So the conflict in the Mississippi is concluded and the River is now in full control of the Union – that portion of the Anaconda Plan is complete.

Union Troops Entering Port Hudson, July 8, 1863
Harper's Weekly – August 8, 1863
(Author's collection)

The Formal Surrender of Port Hudson
Harper's Weekly – August 8, 1863
(Author's collection)

JULY THURSDAY 9 1863
to Day our armies are Celibrating inside of Poart Hudson after a Siege of 45 Days and nights there is grait regoising to Day amongst the Soldiers on Boath Sides General Gardner the Reb is in the hands of
FRIDAY 10
General Banks as a prissoner of war and all officers that was in the foart to Day is very Still our men are Buisey in taking Care of the prissoners and other property in the foart we Soon expect to be on the move home good for that

July 9 & 10, 1863 – to Day our armies are Celibrating inside of Poart Hudson after a Siege of 45 Days and nights there is grait rejoising to Day among the Soldiers on Boath Sides. General Gardner the Reb is in the hands of General Banks as a prisoner of war and all officers that was in the foart to Day is very Still our men are Buisey in taking Care of the prissoners and other property in the foart we Soon expect to be on the move home good for that.

SATURDAY 11

to Day is warm and very muggy
our Regt is up on the Right on
picket Dutey no news of importe
all is Buisey in getting Readey
for to go home which will be a
happy for us all

July 11, 1863 – to Day is warm and very muggy our Regt is up on the Right on picket Dutey no news of importence all is Buisey in getting Readey for to go home which will be a happy for us all.

JULY SUNDAY 12 1863

to Day is Rather a long Day
for me I am in the hospittle
Sick But I am getting Better
all is Still no thundering of
guns nor Rattle of firearmes
Do we hear now

July 12, 1863 – to Day is Rather a long Day for me I am in the hospittle Sick But I am getting Better all is Still no thundering of guns nor Rattle of firearms Do we hear now.

MONDAY 13

to Day is very warm and hot
we hav a good meny in the hospittle
Sick now we hav lost 8 in our
Company now we are all anxious
to Start for home and get out
of this Countrey

July 13, 1863 – to Day is very warm and hot we hav a good meny in the hospittle Sick now we hav lost 8 in our Company now we are all anxious to Start for home and get out of this Countrey.

TUESDAY 14

to Day is warm and they
pass Sloley away we Dont get
much to eat onley water
gruel and hard tack I
am on the gain hope I
Shal be well again Soon

July 14, 1863 – to Day is warm and they pass Sloley away we Dont get much to eat onley water gruel and hard tack. I am on the gain hope I Shal be well again Soon.

ULY WEDNESDAY 15 1863

to Day is warm and plesent our
time of 9 months Expires to Day
By order of Major General
Banks we are free from all Dutey
we think we Shal Start for home
within 6 or 7 Days or So

July 15, 1863 – to Day is warm and plesant our time of 9 months Expires to Day By order of Major General Banks we are free from all Dutey we think we Shal Start for home within 6 or 7 Days or So.

THURSDAY 16

to Day is very hot our Regt
is up on the right on picket
Duty they will Soon moove
into the foart I have not
left the hospittle yet but am
Some better

July 16, 1863 – to Day is very hot our Regt is up on the right on picket Dutey they will Soon move into the foart I have not left the hospittle yet but am Some better.

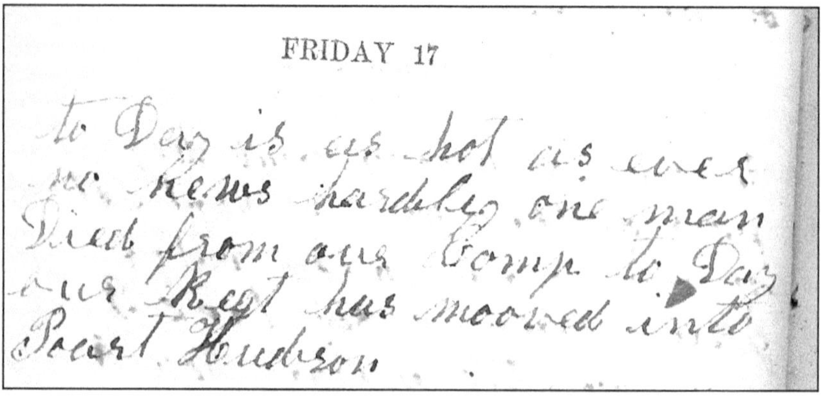

FRIDAY 17

to Day is as hot as ever
no news hardly one man
Died from our Camp to Day
our Regt has mooved into
Poart Hudson

July 17, 1863 – to Day is as hot as ever no news hardly one man Died from our Camp to Day our Regt has moved into Poart Hudson.

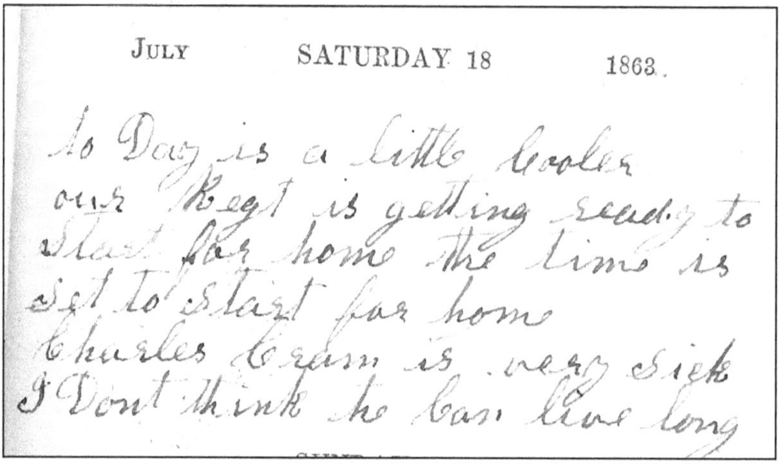

JULY SATURDAY 18 1863.

to Day is a little Cooler
our Regt is getting ready to
Start for home the time is
Set to Start for home
Charles Cram is very Sick
I Dont think he Can live long

July 18, 1863 – to Day is a little Cooler our Regt is getting ready to Start for home the time is Set to Start for home. Charles Cram is very Sick I don't think he Can live long.

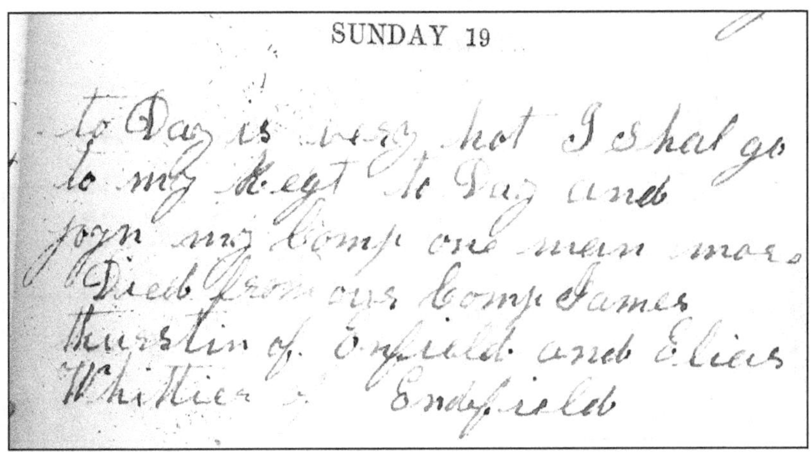

SUNDAY 19

to Day is very hot I shal go
to my Regt to Day and
joyn my Comp one man more
Died from our Comp James
thurstin of Enfield and Elias
Whittier of Endfield

July 19, 1863 - to Day is very hot I shall go to my Regt. to day and join my Comp. one man more died from our Comp. James Thurston of Enfield and Elias Whittier of Enfield.

JAMES C. THURSTON — Co. C

Elias S. Whittier was also from Enfield and enlisted as a private at age 30 and was mustered into Company "C," of the 15th New Hampshire Volunteers on October 8, 1862 – his records indicate that he died of disease on July 14, 1863 at Port Hudson, Louisiana.

James C. Thurston was from Enfield and enlisted as a private at age 18 and was mustered into Company "C," of the 15th New Hampshire Volunteers on October 8, 1862– his records indicate that he died of disease on July 15, 1863 at Port Hudson, Louisiana

MONDAY 20

July 20, 1863 – to Day is very hot I had the Chills last night and am not very well to Day we expect to Start for home next Saturday if not before.

JULY TUESDAY 21 1863

July 21, 1863 – to Day is hot and they Seam a week long I am on the gain now we are waiting paitintly for the time to Com when we Shal get out of this hot and feaverish hole.

WEDNESDAY 22

to Day is a little Cooler Some
Showers no news of eny
importence thare has 3 Boats
arived Et Poart Hudson we
hope one is far us one is far
the 16th N H

July 22, 1863 – to Day is a little Cooler   Some Showers no news of eny importence thare has 3 Boats arived Et Poart Hudson we hope one is for us one is for the 16th NH.

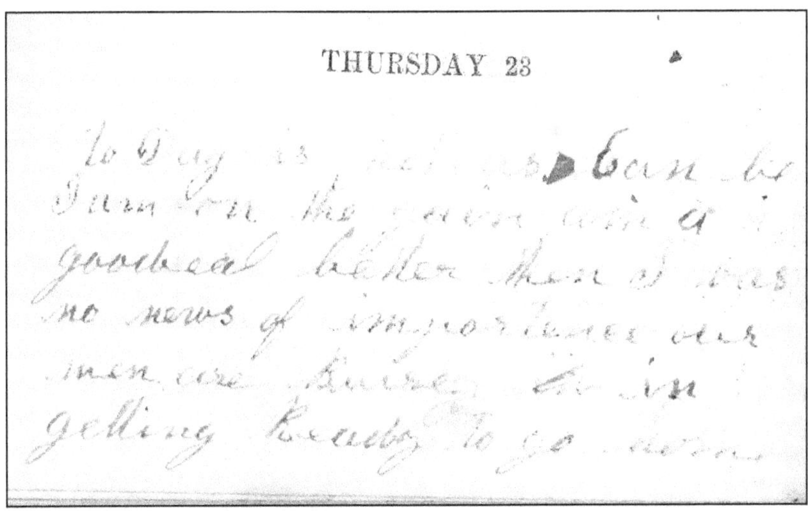

THURSDAY 23

to Day is hot as Can be
I am on the gain am a
goodeal better then I was
no news of importence our
men are Buise in
getting Ready to go home

July 23, 1863 – to Day is hot as Can be I am on the gain am a goodeal better then I was no news of importence our men are Buise in getting Ready to go home.

JULY FRIDAY 24 1863

July 24, 1863 – to Day is a little Cooler there has 4 Regt of 9 months men gon up the River home our turn will Come Soon our Sick is all orderd together Et Pourt Hudson.

SATURDAY 25

SUNDAY 26

July 25, 1863 – To Day is all joy in Camp we hav got orders to go on Boaurd the Boat within 24 hours. Charles Cram died last night was Buried to Day at 11 o clock the 25th 1863 Et Poart Hudson, Louisiana.

So the war was over for Richard and the remaining members of the 15th New Hampshire Volunteers.

McGregor recalls: "July 24, Friday. Very warm; showery toward evening. The Twenty-fourth Maine leaves for home. Preparing to turn over our arms and government property. Major Aldrich made a personal visit to officials at headquarters, and was promised that the regiment should leave for home in a very few days."

CAPTAIN ALDRICH.

Major John Aldrich was born in Franconia, New Hampshire and enlisted on September 16, 1862 as a Captain. On November 3, 1862 he was commissioned into Company "A", 15th New Hampshire Infantry. He was promoted to Major on April 8, 1863 and was mustered out of service on August 13, 1863 at Concord, New Hampshire.

On the twenty-fifth orders were received to turn over all government property and ten day rations were issued for the trip up the Mississippi on the river steamer "City of Madison." At 4 o'clock the regiment marched to a point where all equipments were turned in and all guns except what was needed for a possible emergency. The regiment then marched an additional two miles and at midnight, after a three mile march, the regiment was safely aboard the steamer. The route was first to Cairo, Illinois via the river and then to Concord, New Hampshire by way of the railroad.

The following pages are the final entries in Richard's diary and speak of the voyage up the Mississippi River:

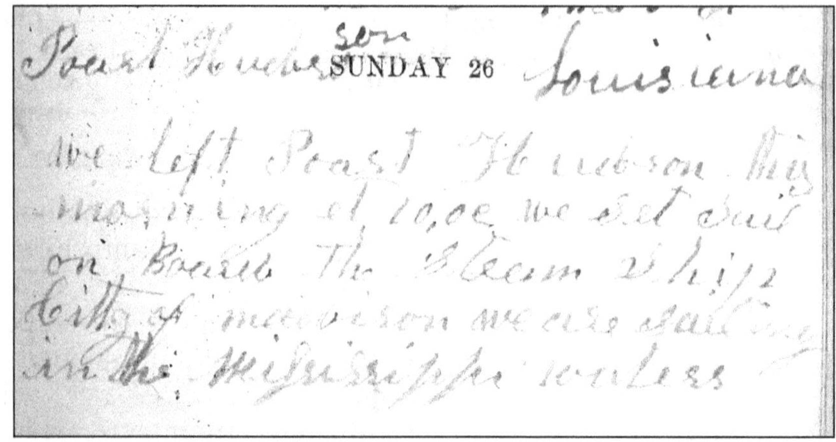
Poart Hudson SUNDAY 26 Louisiana

we left Poart Hudson this morning at 10,oc we Set sail on Board the Steam Ship Citty of madison we are Sailing in the Mississippi waters

July 26, 1863 - we left Port Hudson this morning at 10, oc we Set sail on Board the Steam Ship Citty of madison we are Sailing in the Mississippi waters.

Steamship "City of Madison"

McGregor recalls: "July 26, Sunday. A very hot day, with showers. Farewell, Port Hudson. Great clouds of black smoke ascend from the funnels, and there is a deafening roar of escaping steam from her safety valves, as she stands waiting for the race and trembling in all her frame, when at 9-45 o'clock in the morning the engineer opens wide the steamer's throttle and she begins the ascent of the mighty river."

JULY MONDAY 27 1863

July 27, 1863 - to Day is very hot on the river one of our Soldiers Dyed yesterday and one to Day no news of eny importence we have passed Manaches and Shal Soon be to Vicksburg –

I believe what he is trying to say is that they have passed "Natchez," which is approximately midway between Port Hudson and Vicksburg.

TUESDAY 28

July 28, 1863......to Day is Cooler as we get 3 or 4 miles up the river to Vicksburg we stopped here 6 hours to take on coal one more died on board last night

McGregor writes: "Vicksburg, the Gibraltar of the great Rebellion, was reached at 5 o'clock in the morning, and the steamer lay here till 7 in the afternoon. She crossed the river to coal, and while there a thunder storm and a hurricane of wind arose that swept several boats from their moorings and dashed them about the river, and among them our attendant companion, the 'St. Maurice.'"

WEDNESDAY 29

July 29, 1863 ...to Day is Cool and plesent no news to mention we are still in the waters of the Mississippi

JULY THURSDAY 30 1863

July 30, 1863...to Day is still Cool we are sailing in the Arkansas waters to Day we passed a number of gunboats and also river Boats

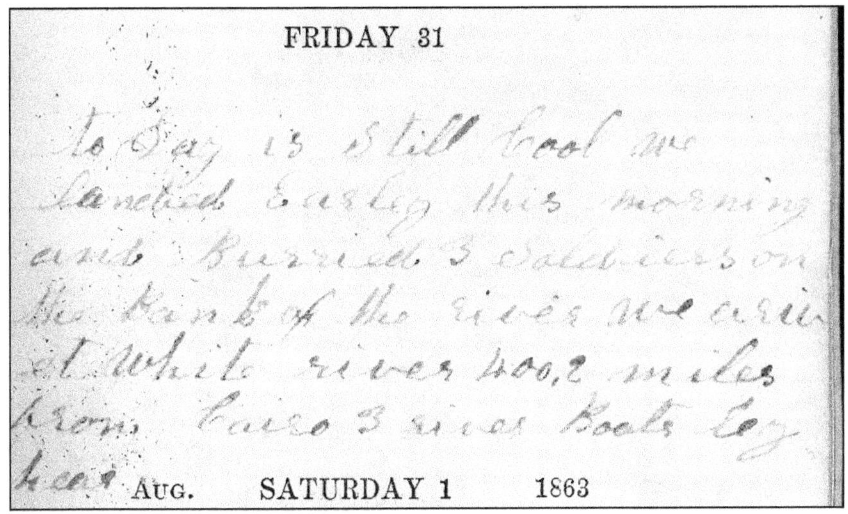
FRIDAY 31

to Day is Still Cool we launched Early this morning and Burried 3 Soldiers on the Bank of the river we arriv at White river 400,2 miles from Cairo 3 river Boats [illegible]

AUG. SATURDAY 1 1863

July 31, 1863......to Day is Still Cool we launched early this morning and Burried 3 Soldiers on the banks of the river we arrived at White River..........

The White River originates in northwest Arkansas and flows in a general southeasterly direction and terminates at the Mississippi River in the vicinity of Rosedale, Mississippi.

The group proceeded up the Mississippi River with numerous deaths along the way and reached Cairo, Illinois, at four o'clock in the morning on August 2, 1863. At this point the troops disembarked the steamer and boarded railroad cars for the trip to Chicago and thence to Concord, New Hampshire, which was reached on August 8, 1863.

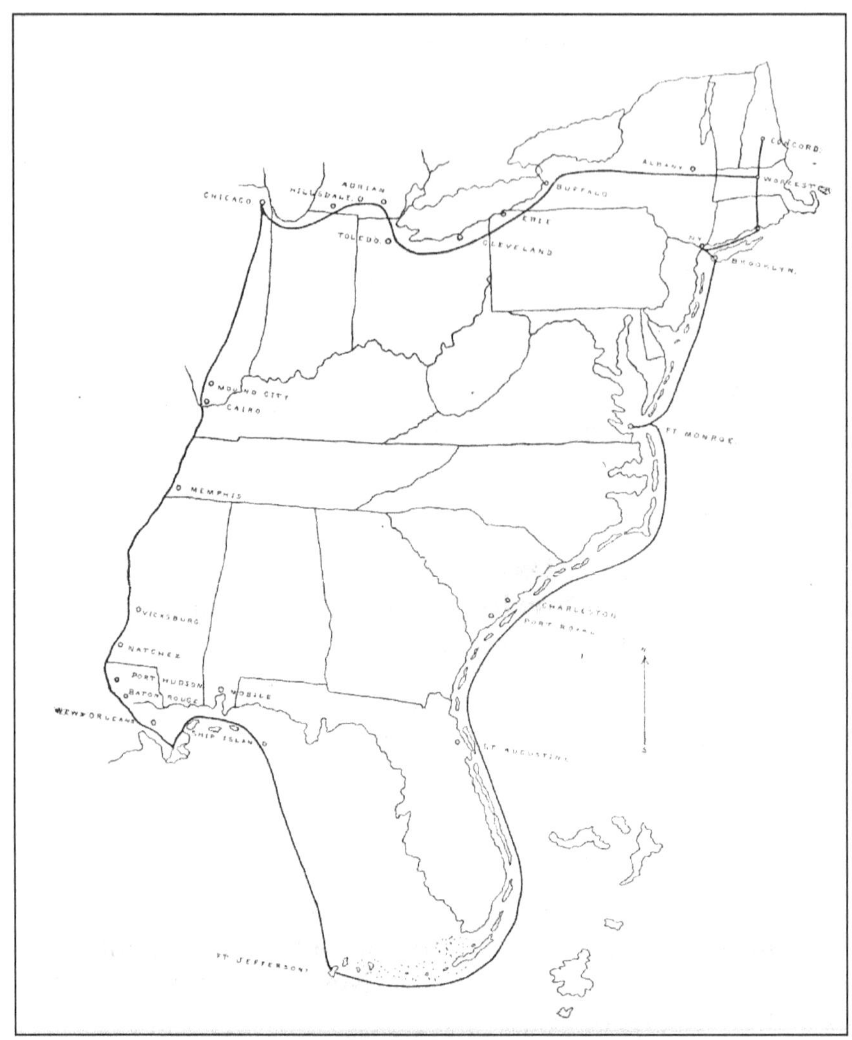

Map showing the route of travel of the 15th New Hampshire Volunteers

The dark line around the ocean portion follows the course of the steamship "Cambria" which ended its voyage at Carrollton, Louisiana. The voyage from Port Hudson to Cairo was via the steamship "City of Madison."

One of the Concord newspapers describes the arrival:

"On Saturday morning, August 8, 1863, between 8 and 9 o'clock, a cannon discharged near the railroad station, announced the arrival of the Fifteenth Regiment, New Hampshire Volunteers. Colonel Klingman. Large numbers of people hastened to the square, and soon the long line of cars were run along side of the platforms in the station, and soon mutual congratulations passed between those inside and outside of the cars. The regiment was in an exhausted condition, and the number of sick large, while several died on the homeward journey. Soon as practicable, the men in marching condition were escorted to camp, and the sick conveyed to the city hall, where a military hospital was soon established, with thirty-five inmates. The people of the city sent supplies, and men and women collected as volunteers to aid in those services of which they had heard so much and seen so little. This is the first ocular demonstration in this city of the effect of a fervid climate and exhausting military services, with all the privations incident to conflict in a distant portion of the country, upon the men of the North, and deepened the already abiding conviction of the extent of the calamity in which the nation was plunged."

At the time the regiment was formed there was a total of 920 men and officers and of this number, twenty-nine were killed, 116 died from disease, sixteen were disabled, twenty-nine deserted, twenty-one discharged, two transferred out, and three, unknown.

When the regiment mustered out of service, the adjutant general's report listed thirty-nine officers and 702 enlisted men; of this total, two officers were on detached service, and 138 men, sick and wounded. The total number of officers and men fit for service at the time the regiment was mustered out was less than thirty-eight officers and 400 men.

Richard returned home and lived in the area until his death in 1921 at the age of 88.

After the war many of the veterans formed associations and organized annual reunions, many were held at Weirs Beach on Lake Winnipesauke. The New Hampshire Veterans' Association was formed in 1875.

In 1884, the Fifteenth Regiment Association elected to erect a headquarters building at the Weirs using contributions from its members and friends. The building was erected in 1888 at a cost of $1,200.

Unfortunately, death takes its toll and the number attending the various reunions diminished as the years rolled on. It is not known if Richard attended any of these reunions, however, a photograph taken at the Weirs Beach headquarters in 1899 shows a veteran who bears a striking likeness to Richard.

This photograph was taken during the reunion of 1899 at the Weirs; the veteran sitting directly in front of the center post bears a striking resemblance to Richard Dodge.

Encampment ribbons were typically distributed to those in attendance, this one is typical and is from 1890, the year after the photograph on the previous page.

(Author's collection)

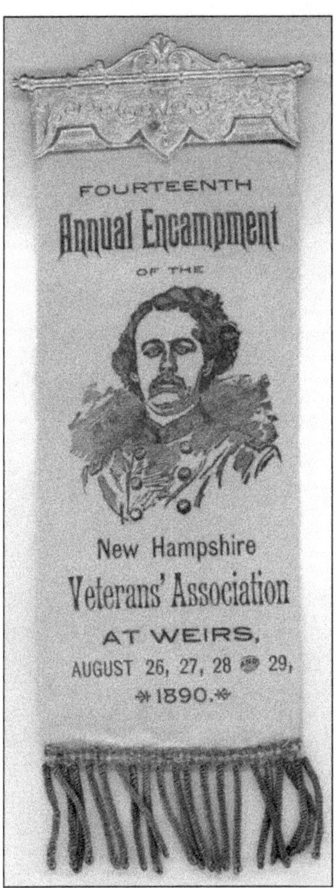

Chapter Eight
Addenda

Addenda – I
Letters from Richard's brother Isaac Dodge:

These letters were written on the 25th of April, 1863 and received by Richard on the 6th of June, 1863:

The letter was addressed to Richard with the address Banks Expedition and in Care of Captain Lang.

Moses Lang was from Bath, New Hampshire and enlisted as a Captain on September 15, 1862. On November 3, 1862 he was commissioned into Company "C" 15th New Hampshire Infantry. He was mustered out on August 13, 1863 at Concord, New Hampshire.

After the war he lived in Bath.

Thirteenth New-Hampshire Regiment.

Camp Suffolk Va the 25
1863.

I will write a few more lines as I
have a few minits more to write
you wanted me rit you I have
to drum if you had bin home a
bout 4 weeks a go you could git in
they have got 2 drumers in the band
and 4 drumers in the regiment but
I thinke you had beter stay till
your time is out you can and I thinke
you can git in and git a good chance
to drum if there is I will write and
let you now it so you can get in if
you wante when you come home I
should like have you come and see me much
you wanted me tell you how I like the
war, I wish to god I was out of it I
should be glad of it I thinke if I git
out of it I den wall it is the damis I
thing that ever was in the world

Thirteenth New-Hampshire Regiment.

Camp Suffork Ap the 25
1863.

Dear Brother I recive your kind letter you
sent me and I was glad to hear from you
and hear that you was well and harty
I am well and hope thes few lines will
find you the same I am harty as a bull
I tuff as a nool I haint ben sick only
to weeks sence I ben in the army I
think I have stood it prety well dond
you fons the hard ships that we have ben
threw we have ben drawn a bout a good
del sence we left, Concord, Dear Brother
I cant stop to writ you all my hard ship
but I will some of it, when we started the
first day of D C the first from the Simany
and com to washington and started from
thair and travel threw meraland to
fort tobacco and went threw to the
river took the steam boat and went to
alquire Creek got off and went to

we was drawn up in a line of batte battle
yestdy they was 10 thousand went out to
drive the rebs back kill 12 and wounded
10 not mutch hurt don but they
trying to case hell all round us
but we watch them like a cat watching
a mouse the most of the Boys is in
good helth now they is diesd out of our
Compy 9 and 10 discharged in our company regiment
only about 6 hundred able four duty made

Charley Packer is wall and harty
as a bull Jonson Clough and Dan Clough
Alby Carter and I camp in one ten
to gether and all well tell Smith
and Charly Clam and Tim galin I
send them my best respects to them
and how do you like to be a shoulger
down in the sunny south I like it
prety wall four I like to shute
at the rebs if you want a good time
Jest come up hear we expect a fight
every day with them if they don they
will be a hard one I tell you now
they is hear now about 40 thousand
still coming in every day

Addenda – II
Diary – Cash Account Section

The following pages are from Richard's diary during his tour of duty in Louisiana:

CASH ACCOUNT—JANUARY.

Date.		Received.	Paid.
1			
2	two bunches of matches		5 cts
3			
4	2 glasses of ale and one lb of shugar		20 cts
5	to one 50 cts bill 3 apples 5		15 cts
6			
7			
8	for washing shirt and drawers		10 cts
9			
10			
11			
12			
13	for apples and [illegible]	75	10 cts
14		45	
15	for [illegible]		15 cts
16	for [illegible] butter [illegible]		35 cts
17	for potatoes [illegible]		42 cts
18	for tea one [illegible]		40 cts
19	for butter and [illegible]		20 cts
20	for ink and mackerell		10 cts
21	[illegible] lbs butter		15 cts
22		190	[illegible] 212

CASH ACCOUNT—FEBRUARY.

Date.	Feb the 1st 1863	Received.	Paid.
	for Brandy 25 and peppermint 20 essence		45
Feb 9th	for soda Crackers		~~45~~
	and for Beer		25
Feb 10th	for ½ lb Butter		20
Feb 15th	for washing Clothes		15
Feb 16th	for Whiskey		20
Feb 16th	for Beer Butter and Cakes.		55
Feb 17th	for one hat		1 25
Feb 19th	for Whiskey		20
Feb 20	for 2 Dinners		25
Feb 21	for Whiskey		20
Feb 25	for fiddle and box		15 00
Feb 25	for one rapier		2 00
Feb 24	for bar for whiskey nuts		1 00
			21 70
Feb 26	for one Rapier		5,00

CASH ACCOUNT—MARCH.

Date		Received.	Paid.
Mar 2	for whiskey		25
Mar 6	for extra and whiskey		2,00
Mar 7	for butter 1 lb		20
Mar 9	for one silk tie		2 00
Mar 10	for 1 wallet		50
Mar 30	for Board and sickness		5 00
	for 3 quarts of Whiskey		1.50
			11.45

CASH ACCOUNT—APRIL.

Date.		Received.	Paid.
Apr 5	of Comp funds	1,00	
Apr 6	for Whiskey and Drinks of Beer &c		1,00
April 10	for 1 qt of Whiskey and Beer and Supper		80
April 22	for 1 qt of Whiskey and Brandy and Beer		1,60
April 26	for 1 pint whiskey 6 lemons 2 Dinners		65
Apr 29	for Beer 2 glases		10
April 30	for Beer 3 glases		15
			4,30

CASH ACCOUNT—MAY.

Date		Received.	Paid.
May 4th	to Mrs Grundy		2,00
5	for cars fare to N. orlens		20
6th	Received from Government		5
	twenty 4 Dollars	24 00	10
15th	to Mrs Grundey		5,00
16th	for Milk Whiskey		50
26th	for Whiskey 3 Pts		1,00
31st	for meals on Steam		
	boat to N. orlens		50
	for Whiskey in		
	Carrollton and		
	3 meals of vidules		1,00
			11.35

CASH ACCOUNT—JUNE.

Date		Received.	Paid.
the 7th	1 canteen of Whiskey		75
Ap 19th	for 1 lb. of Butter		50
the 30th	for 1 lb of onions		20
" 30th	for one Delgream		2,50
" 30	for Whiskey and ginger bread		50
			4.45

Addenda – III
Members of Richard's Unit

MEMORANDA.

Capt Moses Lang

1 Leut Charles Hazilton
2 Leut A. C. Bean
1 orderly Sergt A. V. Cox
2 S D Whitfee
3 John Bishop
4 T. E. Fernald
5 A. G. Spencer
1 Corpl A. V. Parker
2 Benj Bailey
3 H W Howland
4 Austin Morse
5 E. K. Hall
6 John T Dutton
7 A. E. Sweisey
8 A C Rollins
1 Fifer B F Burnam
2 Drumer Richard Dodge
Privats E F Austin
A. K Austin
H S Bailey

H. S. Baker
Danel Bubell
D. S. Butman
C. Bubell
George W. Bailey
C. D. Banks
David Batchelder
H. Chamberlain
Albert Chamberlin
Charles Carber
Richard Clough
Samuel Cushing
Stephen Church
C. J. Carpenter
Charles Green
Wilber P. Cross
John Conaway
C. M. Clough
John Clarke
William H. Dodge
Gibson C. Duth
Ranson S. Day
W. J. Green
E. H. Easbey

L. Mc Emery
Charles B Eales
Gilbert Fuller
Wm W. Farwell
John C. Fuller
James M. Garland
Daniel B Gage
James K Gale
William F. Gillman
Mosby Howland
Henry Howland
Madison Howland
E. B. House
Eben Kentfield
Luther Kimball
Alson Little
E. P. Little
J. B. Lindsey
James H Mullagin
John W. Mullen
John Nelson
Frank A. Oaks
L. C. Place
Myles Pollard

John A. Powers
A. M. Powers
Louis Paradise
Charles H. Proctor
Horace G. Pettingill
Andrew J. Roberts
Isaac Smith
Warren [illegible] Smith
Harvey Smith
Daniel Spooner
William Spooner
John Stuart
Benera Sherman
William S. Stevens
James C. Thurston
Levi S. Terrill
Elias Whittier
John Wilcox
Austin Washburn
William W. Young

Addenda – IV
Members of the 8th New Hampshire Volunteers
Buried at Camp Lewis, Louisiana

Recall that early in his diary, Richard writes about the search for his uncle Joseph Foster's grave, Joseph was a member of the 8th New Hampshire Volunteers, and no doubt Richard recorded these names during his search.

MEMORANDA.

Members of the 8th N.H.V. and their names of those that are buried on Camp Lewis in the State of Louisiana and perish of Jefferson County.

[illegible] Roses of the 8th N.H.V. Comp. A, Died, oct. 26th, 1862.

Stillman Peacock. 8th N.H.V. Co. A, Died, oct. the 23rd 1862.

Danel Hagert. 8th N.H.V. Co. C. Died, oct. the 23. 1862

George [illegible] 8th N.H.V. Died. oct the 25th. 1862.

Joseph Foster 8th N.H.V. Co. K. Died, 1862.

MEMORANDA.

George. B. Willey. 8th. N.H.V
Died. nov. the. 6th. 1862.

Danel. W. Stokes. Comp. F

George. Willey. 8th. N.H.V.
Co. D. Died. nov. the. 6th. 1862.

one unknown Grave
J.G. Whitmore. Died. 1862.

Steven. Hawkins 8th N.H.V
Co. G. Died, 1862

A. Marrows. 8th. N.H.V,
Co. G. Died, nov. 6th. 1862.

D. A. Been. 8th. N.H.V
Co. D. Died. nov. 12th 1862

E.J. Claney 8th N.H.V
Co F Died nov 13th 1862

MEMORANDA.

W. B. Robins 8th N.H.V
Co. H. Died nov the 16th 1862

E. Johnson 8th N.H.V
Co F Died nov the 15th 1862

William Sherry 8th N.H.V
Co. C Died nov the 16th 1862

Charles F. Minot 8th N.H.V
Co H Died nov the 18th 1862

John D. Goodwin 8th N.H.V
Co I Died nov the 20th 1862

D. M. Brown 8th N.H.V
Co. C Died nov the 22. 1862

D. H. Linsey 8th N.H.V
Co A Died nov the 30 1862

MEMORANDA.

Amos B Willes 8th N.H.V.
Co. H Died nov the 28 1862

J. Paifse 8th N.H.V.
Co. H Died nov the 21 1862

Harlen P. Higley 8th N.H.V
Co. I. Died nov the 21, 1862

A. Robins 8th N.H.V.
Co E Died nov the 16th 1862

George M. Avery 8th N.H.V
Co H Died nov the 16th 1862

Addenda – V Martha

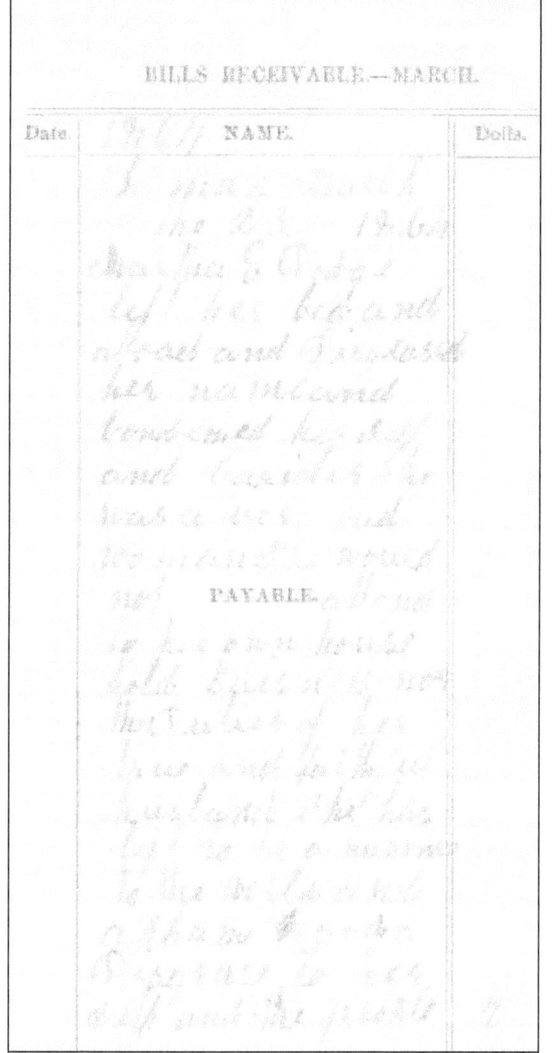

It is unknown at this time who Martha really is. The 1870 United States Federal Census for Littleton, New Hampshire lists a Richard Dodge, age 38 and Martha Dodge, age 27; Richard's occupation is listed as a "saloon keeper" and Martha's as "keeping house." Family members speculate that Richard had been married "three or four times" but the years and names in their records don't agree with census reports. Possibly there is another Richard Dodge, but since he mentions Martha so many times in his diary, that is unlikely. So Martha remains a bit of a mystery.

Addenda – VI
A List of Soldiers Killed and Wounded At Teche Bayou

Richard lists the names of those soldiers that were killed or wounded at Teche Bayou, although he doesn't explain why. It appears that neither members of his Company nor of the 15th New Hampshire Infantry were involved.

Richard's uncle, Joseph Foster, was assigned to the 8th Regiment New Hampshire Volunteers and saw duty in the nearby District of LaFourche in October, 1862, his records indicate that he died later that month. The regiment was part of the expedition to Bayou Teche in January, 1863.so many of the soldiers listed in Richard's diary were his uncles comrades and no doubt died as a result of their duties in the general area of the Bayou.

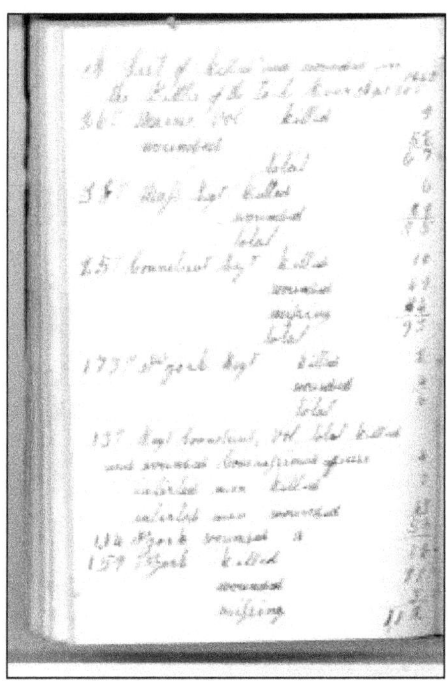

53d Massachusetts Regt
killed 3
wounded 9
12
156 N York Regt
killed 4
wounded 7
11
4th Regt Wisconsin
killed 3
wounded 2
5
8th Regt Vermont
killed Blanchard Co G 1
wounded 7
8
75th Regt N York
killed 2
wounded 14
16
160th Regt N York
killed 2
wounded 6
8
12th Regt Connecticut
killed 2
wounded 14
16
1st U.S. artillery
wounded 10

6th Massachusetts Battery

killed 1

wounded 2

3

1st Louisianna Cavelry

wounded 1

the whole total loss of killed and wounded in 16 Regts is 4,57

Artist Rendition of the Battle in Bayou Teche – January 14, 1863
Harper's Weekly – February 14, 1863
(Author's collection)

THE BATTLE IN BAYOU TECHE.

OUR attentive New Orleans correspondent sends us a sketch—which we reproduce on page 101—of the BATTLE OF CORNEY'S BRIDGE, in Bayou Teche, Louisiana, fought by General Weitzel on 14th January. He had gone up the bayou to destroy a rebel boat called the *Cotton*. The *Times* correspondent thus describes the affair:

Early on Wednesday morning, at 6 A.M., the *Diana*, Captain Goodwin, was ordered to go down the bayou to Lynch's Point, to take the Eighth Vermont across to the left or northern bank, in order for a flank movement on the enemy. At 7 the *Calhoun*, Commodore Buchanan, *Kinsman*, Captain Wiggin, and *Estrella*, Captain Cook, commenced moving slowly up the bayou, and at 9 o'clock reached the formidable obstruction. This was at a place called Corney's Bridge, from a man of that name owning a plantation there. Nothing but the piles of the old bridge remain, protruding about three or four feet above water, and against these the rebels had sunk an old steamer, filled with brick, and placed all manner of rubbish—making it impossible at this time either for the *Cotton* to come down to us or for us to get at her.

At this time, about 8.45, an artillery duel commenced between our gun-boats and the gun-boat *Cotton* and the rebel batteries. The firing continued for some time without any manifest difference to either party. A few desultory rifle-shots had been fired at us from the shore.

Suddenly the *Kinsman* felt something explode under her; it was a torpedo, and her stern was violently lifted in the air, but fortunately with no damage, as was afterward found. An aid of General Weitzel came galloping up to tell the *Kinsman* of another torpedo being planted right ahead, a contraband, escaped from the *Cotton*, having brought the intelligence. Owing to this, and one of her guns being disabled—as the *Kinsman's* officers all assured me—she was cautiously dropping back, after warning both the *Estrella* and *Calhoun* of what had been told her.

Commodore Buchanan, either not hearing or not heeding the information, at once steamed up right ahead of both the *Estrella* and the *Kinsman*, and personally seized the post of danger. It was now about 10 o'clock, when the rebels, from behind their concealed rifle-pits, poured forth a most murderous volley upon our men; and the *Cotton* coming down to attack our batteries, the fight became severe and general.

The gallant Buchanan was one of the first to fall. He was standing forward, spy-glass in hand, a conspicuous target for the deadly missiles of the hidden enemy. W. [illegible] Brown, Acting Chief Engineer, who was near him at the time, having received a spent ball in the thigh, the Commodore said: "Ah! you've got it." The very next moment a ball struck Buchanan in the right cheek, immediately below the temple, passing through to the opposite side. He exclaimed, "My God!" and fell back dead. Some say this gallant officer was rash on this occasion, and threw away his loved and valued life; perhaps so, but it was a rashness which will anchor his heroic name forever.

To show how terribly murderous was the position in which our boats were placed, it is only necessary to state that at this point the bayou was so narrow that the *Calhoun* in turning had her bow and stern aground.

While this was going on our land-forces were by no means idle. The Eighth Vermont, as soon as they had been brought across from Lynch's Point in the *Diana*, at once attacked the rebels in the rear of their rifle-pits, and during a brisk and sharp engagement killed several, took forty prisoners, and put the rest to flight, their [illegible] sending the way. But for this timely and gallant assistance from the Eighth Vermont there can be little doubt that the *Calhoun* would have been lost, from the impetuosity with which the rebels were firing upon her.

In the mean time, no less efficient aid was being given by other portions of our troops. Three batteries—the First Maine, Lieutenant Bradbury; one section of the Fourth Massachusetts, under Lieutenant Briggs, and Captain W. W. Carruth's Sixth Massachusetts—had gone round by the woods from Pattersonville to a point above the [illegible], where they could successfully play upon [illegible]; and in this they were assisted by some of the [illegible] and [illegible] New York, and the sharp-shooters of the [illegible] New York, who played [illegible] among the crew of the rebel gun-boat, which was one of those [illegible] Mississippi steamers, protected by cotton wherever possible, and clad in iron.

Thrice did this ungainly monster retire up the bayou, from the effect of the deadly iron hail poured into her, and twice did she desperately come up to renew the contest. [illegible]

The [illegible] being over, and the ostensible object of the expedition accomplished, our [illegible] and [illegible] returned in perfect order and good spirits.

Addenda – VII
Richard's Military Record

It was rather disappointing that Richard's entire military record in the United States Archives amounted to only two pages:

267

Dodge Richard

Co. C 15 New Hampshire Infantry.

Musician Drummer

CARD NUMBERS.

13809601

13809696

13809784

13809868

Number of personal papers herein

Book Mark:

See also

Age 28 years.

Appears on

Company Muster-in Roll

of the organization named above. Roll dated

Muster-in to date

Joined for duty and enrolled:

When

Where

Period 9 mos.

Bounty paid $ 100; due $ 100.

Remarks:

Book mark:

Addenda VIII
Selected Census Records

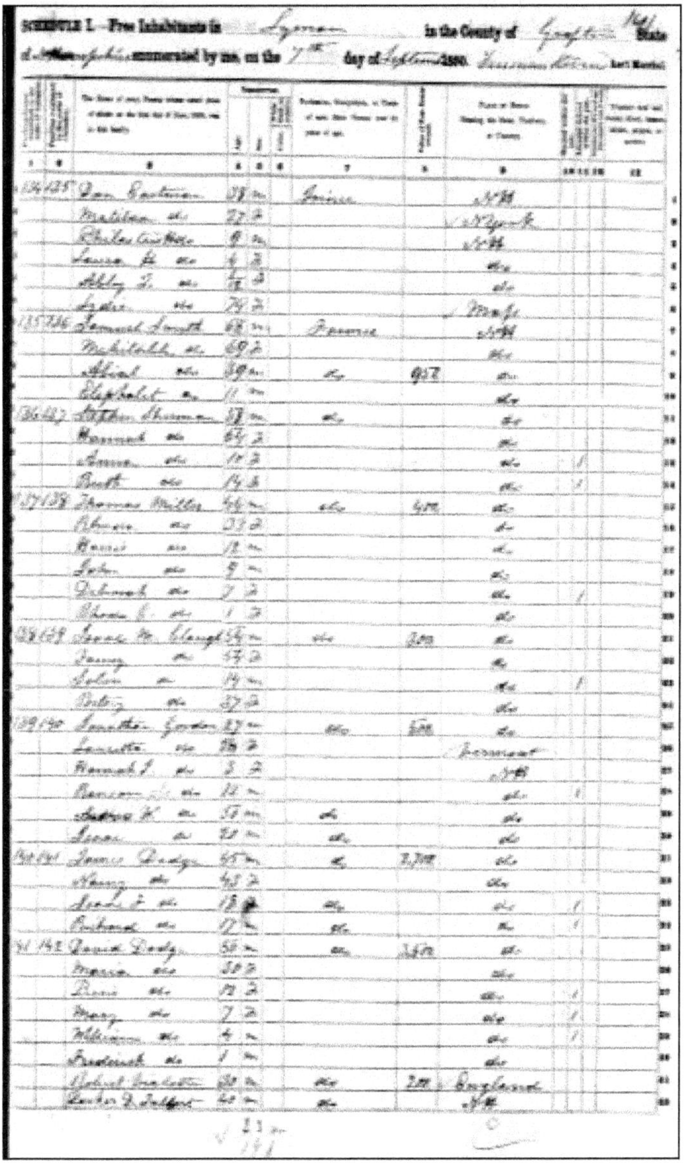

SCHEDULE 1.—Inhabitants in [illegible], in the County of [illegible], State of [illegible], enumerated by me on the [illegible] day of [illegible], 1870. [illegible] Ass't Marshal.

Post Office: [illegible]

	1	2	3	4	5	6	7	8	9	10
1			—— Isaac	21	M	W	Works on farm			Canada
2			—— George	5	M	W	Attending School			New Hampshire
3			—— Fred	2	M	W				New Hampshire
4			[illegible] Martha	19	F	W	Keeping House			Canada
5	[illegible]	[illegible]	[illegible]	23	M	W	Day Laborer	[illegible]		Canada
6			—— Mary	[illegible]	F	W	Keeping House			Canada
7			—— Mary	[illegible]	F	W	Attending School			New Hampshire
8			[illegible]	75	M	W	Day Laborer			Canada
9			—— Mary	[illegible]	F	W	Domestic Servant			Canada
10	[illegible]	[illegible]	[illegible]	[illegible]	M	W	[illegible]			New Hampshire
11			—— Addie	[illegible]	F	W	Keeping House			New Hampshire
12	[illegible]	[illegible]	[illegible] John	[illegible]	M	W	[illegible]	[illegible]		Canada
13			—— Mary	[illegible]	F	W	Keeping House			New Hampshire
14			—— [illegible]	[illegible]	F	W	Attending School			Canada
15			—— [illegible]	[illegible]	F	W	Attending School			New Hampshire
16			—— John	7	M	W	Attending School			New Hampshire
17			—— [illegible]	[illegible]	F	W	At Home			New Hampshire
18			—— Mary	2	F	W				New Hampshire
19			[illegible]	[illegible]	F	W	Domestic Servant			New Hampshire
20			[illegible] Joseph	[illegible]	M	W	Day Laborer			Canada
21			—— [illegible]	1	F	W				New Hampshire
22			[illegible]	30	M	W	[illegible]			Canada
23	[illegible]	[illegible]	Johnson Edward H.	[illegible]	M	W	Deputy Sheriff	[illegible]	[illegible]	New Hampshire
24			—— Ann C.	[illegible]	F	W	Keeping House			New Hampshire
25			—— [illegible]	[illegible]	F	W	Attending School			New Hampshire
26			—— [illegible]	7	M	W	At Home			New Hampshire
27			—— William	4	M	W	At Home			New Hampshire
28			—— Eugene	[illegible]	M	W				New Hampshire
29			[illegible] Jane	[illegible]	F	W	Domestic Servant			New Hampshire
30			[illegible] George	[illegible]	M	W	Day Laborer			New Hampshire
31	[illegible]	[illegible]	[illegible] Cyrus	[illegible]	M	W	Keeps Livery Stable	[illegible]	[illegible]	Canada
32			—— [illegible]	30	F	W	Keeping House			New Hampshire
33			—— [illegible] Cyrus	[illegible]	M	W	Attending School			New Hampshire
34			—— [illegible]	[illegible]	F	W	Attending School			New Hampshire
35			[illegible]	18	M	W	Hostler			Vermont
36	[illegible]	[illegible]	[illegible]	[illegible]	M	W	[illegible]	[illegible]		New Hampshire
37			—— Martha	[illegible]	F	W	Keeping House			New Hampshire
38	[illegible]	[illegible]	[illegible]	[illegible]	M	W	Day Laborer	[illegible]		Canada
39			—— Matilda	[illegible]	F	W	Keeping House			Canada
40			—— [illegible]	[illegible]	M	W				New Hampshire

No. of dwellings 7; No. of white families [illegible]; No. of males, foreign born [illegible]; No. of families 7; No. of white males [illegible]; No. of females, foreign born [illegible]

12,200 — 3500

DEPARTMENT OF COMMERCE AND LABOR—BUREAU OF THE CE[NSUS]

THIRTEENTH CENSUS OF THE UNITED STATES: 1910

STATE [illegible]
COUNTY [illegible]
TOWNSHIP OR OTHER DIVISION OF COUNTY [illegible]
NAME OF INCORPORATED PLACE X
NAME OF INSTITUTION [illegible]
ENUMERATED BY ME ON THE 26th [illegible]

Dwelling	Family	Name	Relation	Sex	Race	Age	Marital	Yrs. married	Children born	Living	Birthplace	Father's birthplace	Mother's birthplace	Year of immigration
127	218	[illegible]	Daughter?	F	W	7?	S				New Hampshire	[illegible]	[illegible]	
127	218	Eastman, Frank	Head	M	W	60	M1	33?			New York	New Hampshire	New Hampshire	
		Hannah E.	Wife	F	W	57	M1	33?		5	New Hampshire	England Eng.	New Hampshire	
		Carl?	Son	M	W	[illegible]	S				New Hampshire	New York	New Hampshire	
128	219	Streeter?, Nelson D.	Head	M	W	88?	W				New Hampshire	New Hampshire	New Hampshire	
129	220	Dowlin?, William	Head	M	W	63	M1	37			New Hampshire	New Hampshire	New Hampshire	
		Martha	Wife	F	W	58	M1	37	1	1	New Hampshire	New Hampshire	New Hampshire	
		Herbert H.	Son	M	W	35	S				New Hampshire	New Hampshire	New Hampshire	
		St Peter, Joseph	Hired Man	M	W	21?	S				Maine	Canada Fr.	Canada Fr.	
130	221	Foster?, Edgar W.	Head	M	W	53	M1	14			New Hampshire	New Hampshire	New Hampshire	
		Susan M.	Wife	F	W	56	M2	14	3	3	Massachusetts	New Hampshire	New Hampshire	
		Faye E.	Daughter	F	W	12	S				New Hampshire	New Hampshire	Massachusetts	
		Douglas H.	Son	M	W	10	S				New Hampshire	New Hampshire	Massachusetts	
		Darwin E.	Son	M	W	8	S				New Hampshire	New Hampshire	Massachusetts	
		Dodge, Richard	Father-in-law	M	W	77	W				New Hampshire	New Hampshire	New Hampshire	
131	222	Ward?, Herbert E.	Head	M	W	44	M1	20			New Hampshire	New Hampshire	New Hampshire	
		Carrie?	Wife	F	W	41	M1	20	4	3	New Hampshire	England	New Hampshire	
		Lillian B.	Daughter	F	W	19	S				New Hampshire	New Hampshire	New Hampshire	
		Gladys A.	Daughter	F	W	14	S				New Hampshire	New Hampshire	New Hampshire	
		Allan? B.	Son	M	W	6	S				New Hampshire	New Hampshire	New Hampshire	
132	223	[illegible], George D.	Head	M	W	30?	M1				New Hampshire	New Hampshire	New Hampshire	
		Edith	Wife	F	W	16?	M1				New Hampshire	New Hampshire	New Hampshire	
		David E.	Father	M	W	60	M2				New Hampshire	New Hampshire	New Hampshire	
133	224	Bigron?, Ira W.	Head	M	W	41	M1	20			New Hampshire	Canada Fr.	Canada Fr.	
		Nina A.	Wife	F	W	36	M1	20	5	5	Vermont	Canada Eng.	New Hampshire	
		James A.	Son	M	W	13	S				Vermont	New Hampshire	Vermont	
		Percy E.	Son	M	W	10	S				New Hampshire	New Hampshire	Vermont	
		Maud R.	Daughter	F	W	8	S				New Hampshire	New Hampshire	Vermont	
		Rachael? A.	Daughter	F	W	6	S				New Hampshire	New Hampshire	Vermont	
134	225	Clough?, George B.	Head	M	W	68	M2				New Hampshire	New Hampshire	New Hampshire	
		Lottie A.	Wife	F	W	53	M1				New Hampshire	New Hampshire	New Hampshire	
		Blake, Myron L.	Brother-in-law	M	W	57	M1				New Hampshire	New Hampshire	New Hampshire	
135	226	Gillis, Hugh A.	Head	M	W	39	M1	9			Canada Fr.	Canada Fr.	Canada Fr.	1894?
		Christina	Wife	F	W	35	M1	9	5	2	Canada Eng.	Canada Eng.	Canada	1894?
		Annie Belle	Daughter	F	W	3	S				New Hampshire	Canada Fr.	Canada Eng.	
		Ronald D.	Son	M	W	2	S				New Hampshire	Canada Fr.	Canada Eng.	
136	227	McNaughton?, David A.	Head	M	W	22	M1	1			Canada Eng.	Canada Eng.	Canada Eng.	1905
		Rose A.	Wife	F	W	21	M1	1	1	1	Vermont	Canada Fr.	Canada Fr.	
		Florence? A.	Daughter	F	W	[illegible]	S				New Hampshire	Canada Eng.	Canada Fr.	
137	228	Callahan, Jerry	Head	M	W	45	M1	5			New Hampshire	Ireland Eng.	Ireland Eng.	
		Nora? E.	Wife	F	W	25	M1	5	2	2	West Virginia	Ireland Eng.	West Virginia	
		Marguerite	Daughter	F	W	3	S				New Hampshire	New Hampshire	West Virginia	
		Agnes	Daughter	F	W	2	S				New Hampshire	New Hampshire	West Virginia	
138	229	Dufresne?, Emmett? R.	Head	M	W	23	M1	3			Canada Fr.	Canada Fr.	Canada	1903
		Alma	Wife	F	W	22	M1	3	2	2	Vermont	Canada Fr.	Canada Fr.	
		Adeline M.	Daughter	F	W	2	S				New Hampshire	Canada Fr.	Vermont	
		Alice R.	Daughter	F	W	[illegible]	S				New Hampshire	Canada Fr.	Vermont	
140?	230	King, Marshall H.	Head	M	W	46	M1	19?			New Hampshire	New Hampshire	New Hampshire	
		Ida	Wife	F	W	45	M1	19?	1	1	New Hampshire	New Hampshire	New Hampshire	

DEPARTMENT OF COMMERCE—BUREAU OF THE CENSUS

FOURTEENTH CENSUS OF THE UNITED STATES: 1920—POPULATION

In October, 2009, I gave a talk to the Lisbon (NH) Area Historical Society that focused on the Richard Dodge diary. After the presentation the following photograph appeared in the *Bridge Weekly* newspaper:

Shown, from left to right – Shirley Peterson and Lillian Guay, both great-great granddaughters of Richard Dodge – me – Sue Carlson and Doreen Kaspszak, both great granddaughters of Richard. I m holding the diary in my right hand and the draft of this book in the other.

I am thankful to Doreen Kaspszak for allowing me to share her great-grandfather with me so that I could share him with my readers.

Chapter Nine
Sources

History of the Fifteenth Regiment New Hampshire Volunteers, 1862-1863 by Charles McGregor, Fifteenth Regiment Association. 1900

The Photographic History of the Civil War In Ten Volumes, Francis Trevelyan Miller, Editor-in-Chief, New York The Review of Reviews Co. 1912.

Campaigns of the Civil War – VIII. THE MISSISSIPPI, by Francis Vinton Greene, New York Charles Scribner's Sons, 1882.

Personal Traces, by Andrea Fitzgerald, Lisbon Area Historical Society, 2005

A Compendium of the War of the Rebellion – Volume III, by Frederick H. Dyer, New York – Thomas Yoseloff, Special Contents of this Edition Copyright by Sagamore Press, 1959

Campfires and Battlefields, by Rossiter Johnson, Gallant Books, Inc., New York, 1960.

The American Heritage Picture History of the Civil War, Richard M. Ketchum, Editor-in-Chief, American Heritage Publishing Co., Inc., 1960

The Third New Hampshire and All About It, by D. Eldrege, E. B. Stillings and Company, 1893

Historical Data Systems, Inc. P. O. Box 35, Duxbury, MA 02331

Frank Leslie's Illustrated History of the Civil War, Mrs. Frank Leslie, Publisher, New York, 1895

The Third New Hampshire and All About It, Daniel Eldredge, E. B. Stillings and Company, Boston, Mass., 1893

Butler's Book, Benjamin F. Butler, A.M. Thayer and Co., Boston, 1892

Sparks from the Camp Fire, Edited by Joseph W. Morton, Jr., Keystone Publishing Co., Philadelphia, 1890

The American Heritage *Picture History of The Civil War*, American Heritage Publishing Co., Inc., 1960

The Mississippi, Francis Vinton Greene, Charles Scribner's Sons, New York, 1882

What a Boy Saw in the Army, Jesse Bowman Young, Hunt & Eaton, New York, 1894

Richard Dodge Diary Annotated
Credits by Chapter

Introduction

Diary – Doreen Kaspszak, with publishing rights

Flag display – Author

Sanitary Inspector's Report – McGregor Page 210

Chapter One

Musket Photos – Wikipedia

Maps – LSU, Special Collections

Army Mail Wagon Photo – Photo.Hist. CW Vol. 8- Page 35

Private Eudy Photo - Historical Data Systems

Cook House Photo – Frank Leslie's Hist of CW – Page 138

Open Air Cooking – Photo Hist. CW Vol. 8 – Page 200

Chapter Two

Bringing in a Prisoner -Campfires and Battlefiels, Page234

2nd Lt. Durgin – Historical Data Systems

Stacked Muskets – Photo. Hist CW Vol. 8 – Page 195

Chapter Three

Photo Studio – What a Boy Saw in the Army – Page 29

General Emory – Historical Data Systems

Transports Awaiting Orders – Photographic Hist. CW – Page 230

Ironclad "Essex" - Wikipedia

The U.S.S. Portsmouth – McGregor Page 251

Chapter Four

Arthur Austin – Historical Data Systems

Benjamin Burnham - Ditto

Hunting Alligators – Civil War in Pictures – Page 44

Chapter Five

Before Active Service – Sparks from the Campfire – Page 50

Grierson Photograph – Historical Data Systems

Grierson's Cavalry – American Heritage *Civil War* Vol. I Page 314

Springfield Landing – McGregor Page 301

Scott's Great Snake – Wikipedia

Enos K. Hall – Historical Data Systems

Pencil Sketch of Port Hudson – McGregor – Page 463

General Grant – General Dow – Historical Data Systems

Lt. Colonel Blair – Ditto

Steamship Iverville – Leslie – Page 378

Chapter Six

Envelope to Richard from Isaac – Diary

Letter from Lt. Perkins – McGregor – Page 445

Bomb and Splinter Proof - History of the Third NH – Page 348

Bomb Proof – Butler's Book – Page 748

USS Ironclad Essex

USS Richmond - Wikipedia

Chapter Seven

James Thurston – Historical Data Systems

Major John Aldrich - Ditto

Steam Ship City of Madison – McGregor - Page 586

Map – McGregor – Page 620

GAR Photo – McGregor – Page 624

Chapter Eight

Captain Lang – Historical Data Systems

www.ingramcontent.com/pod-product-compliance
Lightning Source LLC
Chambersburg PA
CBHW071155160426
43196CB00011B/2089

9781936711055